ENDORSEMENTS

"We all need a sense of purpose and a deeper meaning for our lives. Sometimes, the hardest part in finding this is knowing where to start. Chris Meek found his calling on 9/11, and now he's on a mission to help you find yours, too. In Next Steps Forward, Chris recounts how his desire to give back to those who risked their lives that day has evolved into something much larger: the opportunity for paralyzed veterans to walk again. Chris has written a book that helps you be a person you will admire. The time for self-discovery begins now."

—DANA PERINO
Former White House press secretary and Fox News anchor

"Next Steps Forward is a story of service and sacrifice, of trial and resilience, and of war and coming home. Chris Meek tells a compelling story that will help the American people understand better those who fight in their name. And, it will help American warriors better understand themselves."

—LIEUTENANT GENERAL H.R. McMASTER
author of Dereliction of Duty and Battlegrounds

"As one who served in Iraq with the 101st Airborne, I know the importance of taking action for those who sacrificed for our fellow citizens and our country following the attacks of 9/11/01. In *Next Steps Forward*, Chris Meek chronicles his experiences of that day, and lays out a path of action that every American can follow."

—TOM COTTON
United States Senator

"Chris Meek's book *Next Steps Forward* is as timely as it is inspiring. His personal journey provides an exhilarating narrative on how to do more than remember unparalleled traumatizing events. He helps us realize how we too can flip the script from the helplessness and hopelessness that comes after harrowing events, to uncover our life purpose by actively responding to the pain of others—and by taking small steps at every juncture. Taking next steps forward is one of the strongest antidotes to conquering despair and building happiness. *Next Steps Forward* is a must read for people of all ages who seek direction to build a meaningful life. All we need is to call upon our imagination, courage, and inspiration to take our first step forward. Such acts serve to build better brain health for everyone."

—SANDRA BOND CHAPMAN, PHD
Founder and chief director, Center for BrainHealth

"There are some books worth reading because they dare to have powerful conversations and touch on powerful truths. This is one of those books. It's a must read. Chris is someone whose voice stands out in a sea of voices today, and I'm happy to see him share the truth with all of us."

—CYNTHIA GARRETT
TV host, author, evangelist, and social activist

Beyond Remembering.
The Power of Action.

CHRIS MEEK

Copyright © 2022 by Christopher Meek

All rights reserved. This book or any portion thereof may not be reproduced or used in any manner whatsoever without the express written permission of the publisher except for the use of brief quotations in a book review.

Publisher's Cataloging-in-Publication data

Names: Meek, Chris, author.
Title: Next Steps Forward: Beyond Remembering. The Power of Action / Chris Meek.
Description: Includes bibliography. | Stamford, CT: Chris Meek, 2022.
Identifiers: LCCN: 2022906446 | ISBN: 979-8-9860208-2-2 (hardcover) | 979-8-9860208-0-8 (paperback) | 979-8-9860208-1-5 (e-book)
Subjects: LCSH Meek, Chris. | Philanthropists--Biography. | Businesspeople--United States--Biography. | Leadership. | BISAC BIOGRAPHY & AUTOBIOGRAPHY / Personal Memoirs | BIOGRAPHY & AUTOBIOGRAPHY / Business
Classification: LCC HV27 .M44 2022 | DDC 361.74/092--dc23

1127 High Ridge Road #124
Stamford, CT 06905

www.NextStepsForward.com

Printed in the United States of America

First Printing, 2022

TABLE OF CONTENTS

Foreword: By Kenneth Hersh	ix
Prologue: Why We Remember	xiii
Prelude: "Judge Softly"	xvi
Chapter 1: A Pair of Shoes	**1**
My Own Steps	2
My 9/11/2001	4
Dwelling on My Shoes	10
Chapter 2: Finding My Steps	**13**
Chapter 3: Send Socks!	**21**
Photo Gallery 1	29
Chapter 4: Still Soldier Strong	**37**
Chapter 5: DARPA for Wounds of War	**51**
Exploring the DARPA Model	53
"VARPA" or Veterans Advanced Research Projects Agency	57
Filling the Gap	58
Chapter 6: Fighting Invisible Wounds	**61**

Chapter 7: BraveMind	69
UT-Dallas's Center for BrainHealth	74
VA Innovation Ecosystem	76
Price Tags	77
BraveMind Alliance	79
The BraveMind Program	80
Chapter 8: Reach	85
Forming ReachStrong	91
BraveMind for Civilian Applications	92
Finding New Ways to Communicate	94
Chapter 9: Horizons	95
Horizons for Visible Wounds of War	96
Horizons for Invisible Wounds	98
Photo Gallery 2	103
Acknowledgments	111
About the Author	113
Notes	115

DEDICATION

To Christine Meek: my bride and partner in our journey through life. May each of my next steps forward be alongside you.

And to the memory of Scott Duffy: dear friend and SoldierStrong's co-founder. Without you, this journey would not have started. You guided our strategic development to meet the continually evolving needs of post-9/11 veterans. Your legacy lives on in our work.

FOREWORD

Compassionate. Bold. Vision.

Leadership is obvious from a mile away. Principled leaders prove that one person can make a difference with a compassionate vision that is bold enough to approach problems in ways that others won't or can't. They find solutions that change and improve lives.

Chris Meek has demonstrated this type of leadership throughout his life. *Next Steps Forward* is not just a story, it is an inspiration. It is living proof that one person can make a difference.

Following the cowardly attack on 9/11, a brave cadre of our nation's finest men and women took up arms to protect the freedoms and liberties we enjoy and often take for granted. The nation owes a debt of gratitude to these warriors, many of whom made the ultimate sacrifice. Unique to this battle against terrorism, many returning home brought with them both visible and invisible wounds of war. It is critical that the country embrace these warriors and ensure that they have a successful transition to civilian life—a transition that is healthy and puts them on a path that includes meaningful work and financial security.

NEXT STEPS FORWARD

Chris Meek shares his unique vantage point of Ground Zero and the impact that day had on him. He walks us through his state of mind and how that day motivated him to take action. Inspired by his shoes, something we all take for granted, he mobilized a nationwide effort to send socks to our deployed soldiers engaged in the war. Out of that effort came another goal—to help those who can no longer walk take *their* next step forward. SoldierStrong was born. The mission seemed impossible. But not for Chris and his network of visionaries.

In late 2013, that vision became a reality when Sergeant Dan Rose, a soldier who sacrificed his legs in defense of our freedom, took his first steps in a revolutionary exoskeleton thanks to a donation from SoldierStrong.

But that was just the beginning. *Next Steps Forward* chronicles the marriage of vision, Chris's determination, and evolving technology as it changes lives. In so doing, he has given hope to the tens of thousands of brave warriors who lost mobility in the war on terror. However, Chris's impact didn't stop at just the ability to overcome the physical wounds of war. He found that by helping warriors walk again, he was treating the invisible wounds as well.

Armed with this appreciation, he expanded the aperture of his efforts once again and began tackling the suicide epidemic among our post 9/11 veterans.

It was at this stage in his journey that we met. Chris was selected to be part of the inaugural 2018 class of the "Stand To" Veterans Leadership Program at the George W. Bush Presidential Center in Dallas. That cohort spent six months engaged with a sophisticated leadership curriculum with peers who are all focused on improving veteran outcomes.

Ideas, experiences, and approaches all geared toward the same set of issues proved to be a powerful combination.

The classmates take the curriculum and apply it to their own leadership projects, and put the lessons into practice. They challenge and encourage each other along the way. The goal is to combine lessons and action to amplify the impact of each's work. I will always remember the final session with President Bush where, using SoldierStrong's technology, a wounded vet was able to rise from his wheelchair and walk across the room. The emotion in the room was palpable.

Just like the warriors who have benefited from SoldierStrong's technology, Chris has not stood still. He continues to strive to find new ways to serve our nation's post 9/11 veterans. *Next Steps Forward* will motivate the reader to work harder, set more ambitious targets and never to be satisfied when there is more work to be done.

Get ready to be inspired.

Kenneth Hersh
President & Chief Executive Officer
George W. Bush Presidential Center
Dallas, Texas
March 19, 2022

PROLOGUE

There's an old saying that time heals all wounds. Maybe it's true, but maybe not. Just when we think our visible wounds have healed, we lose people to unseen wounds, such as PTSD, depression, and the lingering emotional and psychological effects of trauma.

Whether we heal or remain deeply scarred, one of the most important things we can do is to remember. This reminds me of another old saying: history repeats itself. Yet, some history must *not* repeat. In fact, the hope of humanity's future requires that we remember in order to ensure that certain history *never* repeats.

But sometimes—many times, in fact—remembering is only part of the story. The other part involves taking action and moving forward—for the lost, the living, those who will inherit the world…and for ourselves.

As the days and months since the attacks of September 11, 2001, become years and decades, collective memories dim. Some wounds have healed. Many have not. If we truly hope for a better future, then we must always remember this day. Beyond remembering, we must also move forward, and be willing to act for the greater good.

NEXT STEPS FORWARD

I remember. I was there. I witnessed the events firsthand from within the shadow of the Twin Towers. I survived. I promised to always remember, and I did. Still, more than 20 years later, I continue to need healing. I know that I'm not alone in this fact. In many ways, the actions I have taken in the last two decades are deeply connected to my own need to do more than just remember.

My survival started when I began taking my next steps forward. Healing began when I started helping others take *their* next steps forward. This story of help and healing—of remembering and acting—is at the core of *Next Steps Forward*.

Honoring the memories of those who lost their lives, the sacrifices of those who served, and the American potential that exists within all of us requires that we continue to remember and learn from 9/11. What's more, we must also act to build a world where every human being has what they need to take their next steps forward.

Whether we've healed, or must yet heal, it is our duty to live up to these ideals. In doing so, we keep alive three of the greatest hopes imaginable:

> One, that this piece of history will never repeat.

> Two, that those who have suffered physical wounds while protecting our nation can take their next steps forward.

> Three, that people who have suffered from any type of trauma can push beyond stigmas, and achieve new mental and emotional strength.

Prologue

After years of trying to bury my personal memories of 9/11, I began using them to build a better world any way I could. I am still on this journey. Perhaps you are on a similar journey as well. My hope is that together, as we take next steps for others and for ourselves, we will win the ultimate triumph.

How far do you want to go? I believe, as Americans, we possess the strength, courage, imagination, and innovative capabilities to go there together.

So let's go. One step at a time.

PRELUDE

"Judge Softly"

Pray, don't find fault with the man that limps,
Or stumbles along the road.
Unless you have worn the moccasins he wears,
Or stumbled beneath the same load.

There may be tears in his soles that hurt
Though hidden away from view.
The burden he bears placed on your back
May cause you to stumble and fall, too.

Don't sneer at the man who is down today
Unless you have felt the same blow
That caused his fall or felt the shame
That only the fallen know.

You may be strong, but still the blows
That were his, unknown to you in the same way,
May cause you to stagger and fall, too.

Don't be too harsh with the man that sins.
Or pelt him with words, or stone, or disdain.
Unless you are sure you have no sins of your own,
And it's only wisdom and love that your heart contains.

For you know if the tempter's voice
Should whisper as soft to you,
As it did to him when he went astray,
It might cause you to falter, too.

Prelude

Just walk a mile in his moccasins
Before you abuse, criticize and accuse.
If just for one hour, you could find a way
To see through his eyes, instead of your own muse.

I believe you'd be surprised to see
That you've been blind and narrow-minded, even unkind.
There are people on reservations and in the ghettos
Who have so little hope, and too much worry
on their minds.

Brother, there but for the grace of God go you and I.
Just for a moment, slip into his mind and traditions
And see the world through his spirit and eyes
Before you cast a stone or falsely judge his conditions.

Remember to walk a mile in his moccasins
And remember the lessons of humanity
taught to you by your elders.
We will be known forever by the tracks we leave
In other people's lives, our kindnesses and generosity.

Take the time to walk a mile in his moccasins.

Written in 1895 by Mary T. Lathrap[1]

Chapter 1

A PAIR OF SHOES

I remember looking at my shoes. Just staring at them and contemplating what had happened a few hours earlier was about all I could do once I finally sat down on the evening of September 11, 2001.

Like every American, I was in shock and utter disbelief. Both words are almost too soft for how I felt, and yet I have none better. In the evening's first quiet moments, it was hard to process what I had literally walked through only hours earlier, one step at a time, along with thousands of other New Yorkers.

I could not find a focal point, or bring my focus to a single idea. My thoughts and emotions were swirling. Between every comforting call I made to say I was safe, I was gripped by the agony of wondering about those who hadn't made it home yet, and possibly never would. Plus, with fears of another attack, the constant news coverage, and the carnage and devastation all around us, it was enough to make even the most disciplined mind spin.

Oddly enough, a pair of shoes—my own shoes—finally grabbed my attention. Of all the things to dwell on, looking at my shoes created the evening's first calm moment. More than two decades later, staring at them is the only peaceful memory I have from the entire day.

NEXT STEPS FORWARD

My shoes had padded and protected every step I took from the American Stock Exchange, near Ground Zero, all the way up Second Avenue to my apartment on the Upper East Side. They only stopped when I stood still and watched an exodus of people walking across the Brooklyn Bridge.

As my mind and thoughts began to settle, I thought about the men and women who took their next steps running *into* the chaos to protect and defend us. In the moment, they were blurs. In reflection, their sacrifices continue to inspire awe.

Alone in my living room, my shoes covered in dust, gravel, and ash, the following realization struck me: we take our next steps forward for granted, right up until we have taken our last step. I thought about all the people who would never take another step again—2,977 people, as we'd learn later. That notion set me, and so many other Americans, on a different path—one of contemplation about how we had gotten where we were, and, much more importantly, how we would get to where we *could* be.

My Own Steps

I had started my career in financial services back in 1995, working for Hull Trading Company, a small, Chicago-based proprietary trading firm. I went to work every day looking for great concepts, companies, and people to invest in, along with innovative ways to help fund the best ideas so they could grow.

Exchange-traded funds were relatively new when I started trading. Our firm was one of the first to use handheld technology on the trading floor. Back then, the idea of "real-time-data" was revolutionary, and our competitors were still trading based on printed price sheets. With the ability to communicate and adapt more quickly than others in the marketplace, we helped revolutionize Wall Street. In 1999, our approach caught the attention of Goldman Sachs. Once they acquired us, I was running floor-trading operations at various exchanges in New York City.

Those were exciting times for a young professional in my line of work. The tech boom was just starting in earnest, and trends in business, technology, and culture would redefine the country and the world. I was proud to go to work investing in an *innovation economy* at the American Stock Exchange, literally in the shadow of the World Trade Center's Twin Towers.

During my years in finance, I've watched brands and products connect us to a brighter future, and make lasting changes in our lives. Apple, Twitter, Google, Facebook, Lucent, Netflix, Uber…the list goes on and on. Truly great brands help us capture and create a future that takes us somewhere new. They connect us to each other, empower our choices, and drive greater access to an economy known for its complexity and emergence.

The economy I'm speaking of recognizes the transformative power of a great idea, product, or company, without regard for the social status of those behind it. It's an economy that opens new opportunities for more people than anything else in human history. Our innovation economy does not demand conformity. Instead, it's built on a desire and drive to connect us to something bigger and brighter. This economy empowers us to *define* our future, rather than having others define it for us—to strive for what we want to become, not to remain stuck where we are.

As a professional, I have had a front row seat as amazing changes take hold. I didn't know it on the morning of 9/11, but my experience of looking for new, revolutionary capabilities and innovations would support me later—seeking revolutionary improvements in physical and mental care for soldiers, veterans, and trauma survivors. It's a powerful and liberating stack of ideas, considering that it came together in the wake of one of history's most despicable acts, which itself originated in a backward corner of extremist ideology, hell-bent on trapping us all in the past.

My 9/11/2001

Like most Americans, I took my next steps forward for granted early on the morning of 9/11. None of us knew how much our lives would change before the day was over.

I arrived at work right around 7:00 a.m., and grabbed my regular order of iced hazelnut coffee and a bagel with cream cheese from the vendor outside of our office building at 111 Broadway. There was nothing out of the ordinary on the day's agenda. I was running floor trading for Goldman, and managed a team of several people on each of three major exchanges. That included two traders and a clerk at the New York Board of Trade, located at Four World Trade Center.

Throughout the summer, the markets had begun to stabilize after the tech bubble's burst. It seems long forgotten now, but the disruption following that burst was a major global economic event pre-9/11.

Our morning meetings occurred early enough to have each trading team ready on their respective floors by around 8:30. Most of any day's trading happened in the first and last 90 minutes of the trading day. At the tail end of the day, we focused on preparing for overnight risk. On the morning of 9/11, I was in a follow-up meeting that went past 8:46 a.m.

A Pair of Shoes

With our office window overlooking historic Trinity Church, our view peered down the stretch of the city known as the "Canyon of Heroes"—the historic ticker tape parade route for astronauts, presidents, and (most importantly) my beloved Yankees. During our meeting, we heard a bang that sounded like a New York City garbage truck hitting a pothole. Steve Rosen, a Goldman colleague, noticed what looked like confetti falling, and said out loud, "I didn't know we were having a ticker tape today."

It wasn't confetti. Instead, embers were falling. We turned our attention to the news that played in the background. Early reports said a small plane had just struck the north tower, One World Trade Center.

The impact of the second plane at 9:03 a.m., followed by an explosion, was unmistakable. A few seconds after hearing and feeling it, we witnessed it nearly live on cable news along with the rest of America. I called our team at the New York Board of Trade, located in Four World Trade Center, and told them to leave. Fortunately, they already had. A number of experienced traders from other firms worked at the same location, and some of them had been there during the '93 bombing at One World Trade Center. They had advised everyone to leave immediately, sensing that something was desperately wrong.

Our building at 111 Broadway shut down the elevators in a state of emergency. Four of us found a fire escape, and made our way down a narrow spiral staircase from the 19th floor. We took turns helping each other. One person in our group had recently undergone knee surgery, and was able to catch one of the last cabs out of the area.

NEXT STEPS FORWARD

I hustled toward the American Stock Exchange, went about one block out of the way, then headed to the corner of Cedar and Church streets. The Twin Towers were immediately visible. I saw gaping holes in both of them, and watched members of Ladder Company 10, some of the first on the scene, make their way into the area.

Glancing up, I caught sight of something that is burned forever in my mind's eye: a woman in a yellow and pink dress falling from one of the buildings. Whenever I have nightmares of that day, this singular memory haunts me. As she fell, she held her dress down in one final act of dignity.

The American Stock Exchange was letting credentialed people in, but not letting anyone out. I entered and began searching for my team of 14 people inside. Like everyone else in the building, they were trying desperately to push out the glass. In that frantic, chaotic scene, I jumped on as many phone calls as I could. My boss in Chicago and I tried to map out a scenario in which the markets would actually open. What would we do? Soon, we were talking about trying to get out of the building.

That's when the news of a plane hitting the Pentagon began to cycle through the crowd.

In that moment, the reality and urgency of being under attack finally hit me. I tried to call my mother to let her know I was okay, but went straight to her answering machine. I tried to call my wife, Christine, but couldn't reach her either. Minutes later, cell service crashed throughout much of Manhattan.

I paced, directed people, and looked for a way out of the building. Odd things happen in moments of such disarray. With adrenaline flooding my system, my focus narrowed into a tunnel—and yet, in the midst of the pandemonium, I spotted my old best friend from kindergarten, John LeMark, a trader for another firm. There we were, spending a few strange minutes together at what seemed like the end of the world.

That's when the earthquake happened. That's what it felt like from the floor of the Exchange when the first tower fell.

It was 9:59 a.m.

AMEX was still not allowing people to leave, but it was clear that their mandate was ill-advised. Four of us—John, Jim Ryan, Evan Thomas, and myself, all from rival firms—found a back fire escape that the building's security wasn't covering. It was at street level on Greenwich, and the World Trade Center was half a block to the north. We took the opportunity to leave, pushed our way out, made a left turn—away from the wreckage—and began walking.

The thick white and gray ash was stifling. I could only see about six feet in front of me. It choked our lungs, burned our eyes, and compounded the confusion that was happening all around us.

By now, there was no cell coverage anywhere, and no way of getting news. Overhead we heard what sounded like fighter jets. Were they ours? We had no way of seeing or knowing what was happening, or what would happen next.

My escape plan began to map itself out in my head: turn left, go straight until we reached the Staten Island Ferry terminal, then turn left again to hug the FDR. If those jets belonged to some other nation or entity, we could at least jump into the East River and take cover.

NEXT STEPS FORWARD

As soon as we started walking, we saw more and more heroes rushing into the chaos. New York City Police, New York City Fire, EMS, Metro Transit Authority. They all just kept coming and coming. These too became impressions that remain burned into my mind forever. They also point the way to a debt I don't believe I will ever be able to repay.

Less than a half hour into our walk, we felt another tremor. The second tower collapsed in the smoke.

It was 10:28 a.m.

We walked along the river among an ever-growing mass of people, each of us struggling in our own way to put one foot in front of the other. We could have turned on each other, and let our panic get the best of us. That never happened. We were all New Yorkers, all Americans. Mutual aid, compassion, and care became the norm without any of us thinking otherwise. Strangers helped each other, held hands, pitched in to lighten loads. In the face of the worst possible terror, the best of humanity rose to the top of our experience.

When we reached Fulton Fish Market, workers handed out wet paper towels so we could clean soot from our eyes. People searched for their friends, coworkers, and family members they were worried about. Jim Ryan was the first of our group to reach his apartment in Stuyvesant. He wrote down phone numbers and promised to call our spouses from his landline so they knew we were safe.

By the time we reached NYU Hospital, we were out of the cloud. Whatever wind blew that day went north to south, which helped to clear some of the smoke. Only a few hours after the first plane struck, people were already pinning pictures of the missing to fences and walls.

When I made it home, it was early afternoon. My emotional state wavered between happy and numb, grateful and grave. Just hugging Christine, who'd gotten home before me, filled me with something beyond joy.

I needed to call people to let them know I was okay. I stashed myself in the bathroom, the only place in our apartment where I could have a private conversation, and called my in-laws first. They lived in Castleton, New York, just outside of Albany, but were away in Colorado Springs. No one knew when airlines would resume flights. As much as they were worried about getting back, they let me talk for as long as I wanted, listening thoughtfully as I told them about the smoke, the people, the sounds, the steps. I kept shifting the conversation back to their situation.

"There's no way you're getting on a plane anytime soon," I said. I offered to drive out to get them, but they declined. They said they would figure it out.

The last person I called was my mother. Unlike my call with my in-laws, talking with my mother was full of silences, long pauses, and sighs. Some sighs evoked relief, others worry.

"I'm fine, Mom," I kept hearing myself say. "I'm fine."

"I know you are," she said. "But I'm worried about what happens next."

"Me too."

Dwelling on My Shoes

> *"A great people has been moved to defend a great nation. Terrorist attacks can shake the foundations of our biggest buildings, but they cannot touch the foundation of America. These acts shatter steel, but they cannot dent the steel of American resolve. America was targeted for attack because we're the brightest beacon for freedom and opportunity in the world. And no one will keep that light from shining. Today, our nation saw evil—the very worst of human nature—and we responded with the best of America. With the daring of our rescue workers, with the caring for strangers and neighbors who came to give blood and help in any way they could."*

President George W. Bush, from his Oval Office address, the evening of September 11, 2001

President Bush's words filled my ears and continued to echo around our apartment long after his speech was over. I had witnessed the substance—both good and evil—of which he spoke.

It was hard to sit still that evening and all through the night. I knew I needed to rest, get out of my clothes, find a way to start to unwind. But I couldn't. I was on the hunt for information, anything I could find—TV, radio, internet, neighbors. Yet, no matter what I found, heard or saw, everything felt hollow.

That's the moment I finally started to focus on a single image: my shoes. When I forced myself to sit down and take them off, it struck me. The dust and ash that covered them wasn't just rubble from buildings. Within that dust and ash were the remains of men, women, and children who had been murdered indiscriminately. They'd taken their last steps on earth earlier in the day without knowing those steps would be their last.

When I woke up on September 12, 2001, my shoes were right where I left them, still covered in the history I'd walked through the day before. On September 13th, they still hadn't moved. Days and days, weeks and weeks, finally more than 20 years later, I have not cleaned those shoes. I never will. I look at them every day and remember the people who died on 9/11, as well as those who have given their lives in defense of our country since. I do it to remind myself that the steps I take are for them.

Going back to that evening, and in the first few days that followed, I felt the beginning of an urge to move forward for others. I didn't know what those steps would look like, or how I would take them, but I knew that my calling in life was about to shift. I would eventually find a way to help others take their next steps forward.

That simple realization changed my life. In some ways, it saved my life.

Chapter 2
FINDING MY STEPS

It took years, in fact decades, until my path forward began to form—and for me to gain enough experience that I felt I was ready to share something valuable with the rest of the world.

First, in the days that immediately followed 9/11/01, I focused on doing everything I could to get the markets ready to reopen. I felt fortunate that I could lose myself in very focused, pinpoint steps and chores. The sense of urgency fed my adrenaline, which was exactly what I needed at the time to tap into meaning and purpose.

The attacks happened on a Tuesday. The markets were closed the rest of the week, and reopened on Monday, September 17th. Part of strategizing their reopening involved heading back to Ground Zero, which was a searing experience.

No doubt, every American who was alive then remembers the images from those awful days. I'm sure even those who were not born have seen pictures and videos from the smoldering wreckage. When I close my eyes now, it's not the sights I remember, but the smell: burning asbestos. Even as crews removed remains and debris, the smell seemed to linger forever.

But again, I was lucky to be able to put my head down and focus on doing my part to support the markets. Like nearly

NEXT STEPS FORWARD

every American at the time, I felt like I had a role to play to make sure terrorism did not shut us down for good. Our nation was wounded, but we were far from dead.

Our first few days of work were 20-hour marathons complete with checking off task after task—fueled, focused, and fully alive. On the surface, the tasks themselves were mundane: purchasing laptops so people could work in new locations; getting our T1 line up and running; connecting with everyone on my team to make sure they were okay coming back to work. But there was nothing mundane about the goal: to get up from the mat and keep the nation moving forward.

The most powerful, difficult, and awe-inspiring chore: actually getting on the subway to go downtown, only to come out at street level and walk by Ground Zero every day.

We had to move the AMEX into the NYSE basement to get back to operations. At Goldman, we had no T1 lines, no computers, and very few other basic operational resources from our previous office.

I stopped by The Wiz, a classic New York City electronics store in my neighborhood on the Upper East Side. My plan was to collect whatever computers they had available. I left with four Sony laptops, which became our only infrastructure for a period of time.

As I walked out, Lee Kranefuss called me on my mobile and asked how I was doing, and if we would be open for business on Monday. Lee was the CEO of Barclay's Global Investors (later acquired by BlackRock). They had started iShares about 18 months earlier. It was a critical time for his suite of ETF products, and he needed to know what was happening.

As we started to piece things together, there were ceaseless reminders that we were in a new, highly uncertain reality. The Brooks Brothers space across from our office had become a makeshift morgue. There were several evacuations for potential bomb threats—thankfully false alarms. The week we reopened, the anthrax scare began. Multiple poison-laced letters were circulating to high-profile leaders and media personalities around the country. The idea of anthrax in the mail only compounded the fear and confusion the entire country felt.

Still, we opened. Markets resumed trading and, in a show of American resilience and determination, before the year ended, the Dow exceeded pre-9/11 levels. It wasn't always smooth, of course. On Monday, September 10th, the Dow closed at just over 9,600. On the 17th, it closed nearly 700 points lower. The bottom came at the end of that first week, when the Dow closed at just over 8,235. But that was indeed the bottom, and on the last day of the year, the Dow closed at 10,021.57—a remarkable run, and a true sign of resiliency to say the least.[2]

For every positive memory that involved the market, there were others mixed in that still bring me back to the reality of life taking place outside. There was a bar called Suspenders[3] right at 111 Broadway, a classic watering hole where New Yorkers of all stripes gathered for friendship and refuge. The founders had all been firefighters, and inside it was impossible not to run into a first responder or recovery worker who had a story from Ground Zero—some hopeful, some grim. I was always in awe of them—I still am, just thinking about them.

Seeing them always took my thoughts backwards to those first moments when I began walking away from the wreckage, and when many of these very same people were rushing toward it. How could any of us ever repay those men and women? What part did we each have to play in caring for those who bore the brunt of the sacrifice, and in building a better tomorrow?

As the days turned to weeks, the same questions immediately applied to those who would fight the war on terror. The way life began to stack up was almost too bizarre for me to handle. Coupled with my work-place focus, and happy but melancholy moments in Suspenders, my life was changing as well.

Two weeks after 9/11, Christine and I were packing boxes and moving to Stamford, Connecticut. We'd been planning it for some time, had gone through all of the prerequisite steps as we closed on our first home, and yet the timing was almost baffling. From one way of looking at it, we were taking our next steps as a couple, and eventually as a family. But from another, there was a pang of guilt in me, as if I was somehow abandoning the city. Such were the mental games I found myself playing in certain moments of quiet.

Then, on October 7, the first American forces began fighting in Afghanistan. We worried about them, but felt a great sense of pride for those who were taking this righteous fight to the cowards who had murdered our innocent civilians.

As the year went on, it felt as if Americans from every corner of the country continued to pour whatever they could give into supporting one another—always with special focus on those who had lost someone or something on 9/11, during the recovery, or in the fight. Small things. Big things. Blood drives. Picking up bar tabs for strangers. Holding doors. Thanking men and women in uniform for their service.

Recognizing heroes on the police force, in the fire station, even in the post office as the anthrax scare lingered. People wore pins on lapels, hung flags outside their homes, cheered President Bush like never before when he threw out the first pitch in Game 3 of the World Series. The attacks had brought us closer, and, as a nation, we felt as if we were truly in everything together.

Yet, the idea of just writing a check seemed terribly impersonal to me, especially considering my own experiences that day. Even if I'd picked up every firefighter's tab in Suspenders for a decade, I'm not sure it would have scratched the surface of what I was feeling. I knew I owed so much more than a thank you and a pat on the back, but I didn't know what it was, or how to get started. I was stuck looking for the right steps to take.

Time is a funny thing. One moment, Christine and I were settling into our new home, toasting glasses of wine in a kitchen filled with packing boxes. The next moment, six years had gone by. We were the parents of two small children, comfortably set in our routines.

The country went through a lot between the end of 2001 and the spring of 2007. That's around the time that the first ripples of the coming financial crisis started making their way to shore. For many of us, especially those who had lost someone on 9/11, or in the war effort that followed, the wounds of the terrorist attacks were still fresh, and the scars would never go away. However, the spirit of togetherness and unity I remember feeling in the fall of 2001 had become something else. Bickering. Finger-pointing. Politicizing.

Despite the years, the new home, and the new circumstances of fatherhood, I continued to feel the urge to do something...to give back to those who had given so much. Over time, I shared this feeling with colleagues, many of whom felt the same way. One person who listened quite a bit was Chris Munger, a former Marine and FBI agent who had become a close friend. Chris lived in Stamford. He was a little older than me, and often when we talked, he'd switch gears between friendly banter and fatherly advice without blinking an eye.

Like me, Chris was also frustrated at the fact that charitable money didn't always wind up going to the people who actually needed it. We weren't naive to the fact that charities had overhead, expenses, marketing budgets, and salaries to pay. We wanted to do something that was more direct. Plus, even though most charitable giving happened with the best of intentions, many efforts we knew of seemed focused on victimhood. We wanted to do something that would empower, but couldn't put a finger on the solution.

This problem in my mind had simmered off and on since 2001, and went back to a boil when the financial crisis hit. By late 2008 and early 2009, I saw people losing their homes and livelihoods. I knew that if I continued to wait until I had *the perfect idea*, I'd stay stuck—nothing more than a spectator on the sidelines. So I did the opposite: I stepped into the fray.

At the very least, I knew that I could apply what I had seen work in the economy to the things that weren't currently working. I wasn't fully prepared, but I was compelled. I let that motivation guide me.

With the help of a few friends and an iPhone, we launched an organization called START Now! In many ways, the acronym said it all: Start Taking Action and Responsibility

Together. To me, and to many others as I'd soon discover, taking action together was what everything was all about.

Our organizational mission was direct: to help people and families become self-sufficient through education, support, and opportunities that were readily available to them. We opened doors and created change at the community level with events, training, and workshops that helped people build financial literacy and new skills they could use to get back on their feet.

If START Now! sounds big and well planned, let me back up a bit. In the beginning, it wasn't an organization at all—it was an event we hosted in April 2009 that focused on loan modification. I used my industry connections to get five banks there, plus a few agencies that offered foreclosure assistance. When it was over, 36 families from the Stamford area were able to modify their mortgages, avoid foreclosure, and keep their homes.

That single event soon led to others, which led to others. In May, we formally launched START Now! as a 501 (c)(3) organization, and continued to host events and workshops in the months that followed, all through the financial crisis. Eventually, we helped more than 250 families avoid foreclosure.

It's hard to explain the power of an experience like that. For a moment, consider any community in the United States right now. What would it mean if, by the end of the night, or the week, or the month, a dozen, or a hundred families were able to keep their homes? What would it mean if they were able to sleep better, knowing that tomorrow, they wouldn't have to worry about paying their bills, or deciding between paying the mortgage, buying groceries, and making sure they can afford medications they need?

NEXT STEPS FORWARD

The galvanizing energy of START Now! began to calm the restlessness I'd felt for nearly a decade. In the process, it had a clarifying effect on my thinking: if a community of people could do this, what else could we do? What was the *next* step? That answer came when Chris Munger called me one evening in the summer of 2009.

Chapter 3
SEND SOCKS!

"Send socks!" Chris said into the phone. I could hear the excitement in his voice.

"Excuse me?" was the only thing I could think to say in reply.

"Socks!"

"I heard that part," I said. "But what are you talking about?"

As always, Chris had it right. It just took me a moment to catch up. He had received a letter from Marine Sergeant Major Luke Converse, who was leading forward-deployed Marines in Afghanistan.

In the letter, Sergeant Major Converse mentioned that his troops had all the military advantages they could ask for: the best training, weaponry, intel, support…yet they were missing some simple but important personal items. For one, they didn't have enough water to drink, let alone take a shower or wash their clothes. Consequently, they were running out of things like clean tube socks. They'd wear pair after pair until they ran out, then start a new pair. But now the sock rations were low.

NEXT STEPS FORWARD

"And baby wipes," Chris said.

"Baby wipes?"

"'Sheets of gold,' according to Sergeant Major Converse," he said. "Hygiene, Chris. They don't shower for days. Baby wipes are the next best thing."

Socks and baby wipes. I couldn't help but shake my head. Back in '09, our military budget was already north of $700B, and yet our troops lacked the most basic supplies.

The next time I saw Chris, he shared Sergeant Major Converse's letter with me—seeing his words on paper was even more impactful than hearing Chris read them over the phone. That night, I sat in my living room, and found my thoughts drifting to the dust-covered shoes I'd tucked away in my closet. Suddenly, all of my memories from 9/11 began to flood back. I closed my eyes and literally saw every step I took that day. Eight years! How could it be that so much time had gone by?

Socks and baby wipes? I couldn't stop shaking my head, but here it was: a chance to help those who were fighting to prevent another 9/11 from ever happening take their next steps forward with a little more comfort.

I decided that sending socks to those on the battlefield would be my next step forward, and our organization's next step as well. True, it wasn't the most glamorous idea, but it was a small way to make a dent in a much bigger problem.

Scott Duffy, a close friend and colleague from Goldman Sachs, shared my desire to do something more direct and meaningful to support our troops. He'd also been in the area of Ground Zero on 9/11, and when I mentioned Sergeant Major Converse's letter, he didn't hesitate. In that moment, SoldierSocks was born: a 501(c)(3) charitable organization that would directly respond to Sergeant Major Converse and every other similarly situated unit we could find.

A couple of days later, we drove around to pick up supplies—wipes from a nearby pharmacy, then socks from a sporting goods store. When we told the businesses what we were up to, they didn't hesitate either—they matched our donations with their own.

Soon after, the community began pitching in, and the response was overwhelming. More and more local businesses, schools, churches and synagogues got involved—places like Reveal Hair Salon, New Balance, Vineyard Vines, and others joined the effort with direct donations. Throughout Stamford, elementary schools, fire, and police departments all pitched in to organize and prepare supplies for shipment.

As people, businesses, and organizations jumped in, even more came to help. It had a wildfire effect, which was great, but soon we had a new logistical worry: how would we actually ship everything to a war zone?

A volunteer introduced us to Marine Aviation Logistics Squadron 49, and the Air National Guard at Stewart Air National Guard Base in Newburgh, New York. They had all the ins and outs we needed to ship, and when we were ready, they took the supplies we'd gathered directly to Afghanistan. Six weeks after we started our effort, our first shipment—nearly 1,500 pounds of supplies—were en route to deployed troops.

NEXT STEPS FORWARD

That wasn't the end. In fact, it was just the beginning of what SoldierSocks would become.

Friends, neighbors, Scout troops, and even elected officials began to join in. Connecticut Lt. Governor Michael Fedele attended one packing session. So did Congressman Rob Simmons—a retired US Army colonel. Soon, I didn't even recognize most of the volunteers who showed up. And the flood of new people continued.

Stamford-based Conair began providing boxes and tape, which were getting harder and harder to come by as SoldierSocks grew. By then, our first round of supplies, which fit snugly into the back of my old Ford Explorer, was a distant memory. We'd up-leveled to needing 24-foot moving trucks, plus 10 people at the airbase to unload for over an hour.

Our collective feeling of shared and meaningful success was palpable. Yet, I began to wonder whether or not we'd achieved the goal of our project, and if it was time to move on. Was this a finite situation that had reached its "Mission Accomplished" moment? No, because the mission *was not* accomplished—not by a longshot.

More and more requests came in, and continued to do so for years. Some came from concerned family members back home, others from total strangers who wanted to pitch in. Some even came from troops in the field of combat.

Verda Reeves, whose son, Sergeant Seth Holland, was serving in Helmand Province, wrote and explained that the combat support hospital was close to the action. They needed the same kind of support we were sending to

Send Socks!

deployed troops: socks, wipes, and other basic necessities. In this case, it wasn't just for hospital personnel, but for the wounded as well.

People throughout Stamford, as well as colleagues in New York, remained supportive, and wanted to do more. I knew, however, that our capacity was limited to what we could source from local stores, what our volunteers could package, and what my garage could actually hold between shipments. Things became a little more interesting when winter's first freeze came, and we couldn't park our cars in the garage because it was full of supplies. Thankfully, Christine's commitment never wavered.

We were reaching some very real limits, and didn't know how we would accommodate new requests. This created a paradox, as the stress of *not* being able to fulfill some requests began to weigh on us. That's when the press we'd received up to that point turned into something bigger: *Elvis Duran and the Morning Show* invited us on their program.

If you're not familiar with the show, it's based in New York City, syndicated in 75 markets across the country, and boasts 8 million weekly listeners. I'm a financial services person, not a media personality—and I certainly was even less of one back in 2009. I had been an avid listener and fan of the show for years. Needless to say, I was more than a little nervous to go on national radio.

Thankfully, Duran was a pro. As a New Yorker who lived through 9/11, he was deeply committed to the cause. In fact, he was sensational during our time on the air. He put me at ease, allowed me to tell our story, and opened vast new possibilities for our effort.

NEXT STEPS FORWARD

After the program, things got even more exciting. Within days, people were holding drives for our cause from Maine to Miami, Austin to Hollywood. Now we would have more than enough supplies to cover each request that came in from deployed units.

In addition, businesses from around the country began to respond. Even Connecticut-based World Wrestling Entertainment (WWE) joined the effort, initially helping with three, 500-pound pallets of donated goods: sunflower seeds, vitamin water, flavor packets for bottled water, beef jerky, branded hats and tee shirts, DVDs, and more.

The Connecticut legislature hosted a sock drive at the state capitol building in Hartford. Senators Joe Lieberman and Scott Brown aided the efforts. Over the days and months that followed, many more joined as well, including *Sports Illustrated* magazine and Cablevision, both of which provided critical public exposure.

American Airlines began providing corporate support in the form of free airfare for certain events. Dinosaur Bar-B-Que sponsored a "Sauce for a Cause" promotion, giving all proceeds of their co-branded Sensuous Slathering BBQ Sauce to the effort.

Partnerships continued to roll in: Specialty Freight Services, the Fraternal Order of Eagles, S&P Global, The Wawa Foundation, Multistack, Total, Operation Hat Trick, Horizon Media, General Dynamics, Honeywell, GE Foundation, and Rosati Ice to name a few. Each contributed in whatever way they could, some in-kind, others with cash as our programs developed and evolved. Each one made a meaningful difference, and helped make next steps possible for those who were serving.

Send Socks!

By 2014, around the time that major combat operations started to wind down, SoldierSocks had delivered some 75,000 pounds—roughly 37 tons—of supplies to 73 deployed units in Afghanistan and Iraq.

Years after I had first read Sergeant Major Luke Converse's letter, he and I had the chance to meet. His first words to me were "thank you." Yet, I couldn't help but think that he had it backwards—I was the one that should be thanking him. He, like so many others, had given so much to this country. Not only were they the true heroes, but their service had effectively given me the direction and purpose I'd been struggling to find, especially as I yearned to give something back.

After meeting Sergeant Major Converse, I found myself once again dwelling on the shoes I'd worn on 9/11—on the ash they were still covered in, and the never-ending toll of that day. In a certain way, Sergeant Major Converse had helped me step back into them. His written words had prompted me to do something, and the act of stepping forward had put me in touch with hundreds of other people who felt the same way. I saw a path begin to form, a sign that read "this way forward."

Photo Gallery 1

Chris Meek with United States Senator John McCain on the floor of the New York Stock Exchange on September 17, 2001, the first day markets opened after the terrorist attacks of 9/11.

NEXT STEPS FORWARD

SoldierSocks donations prior to our first shipment. Summer, 2009.

SoldierSocks donations prior to our second shipment. December, 2009.

Photo Gallery 1

Chris Meek and his two daughters gather grassroots donations in support of deployed military troops ahead of another shipment. Summer, 2010.

Chris Meek hosts a packing party in his driveway. Connecticut Lt. Governor Michael Fedele joins the effort as a volunteer (left, in black t-shirt). Summer, 2010.

By 2011, SoldierSocks began to gain quite a bit of notoriety. Above, Chris meets with Jimmy Fallon of Saturday Night Live and Late Night fame.

Chris Meek presents Elvis Duran the 2015 Commitment to Service Award outside of Duran's broadcast studio.

GROUND ZERO

4 WORLD TRADE CENTER

FDNY TEN HOUSE

BROOKS BROTHERS

CANYON OF HEROES

AMERICAN STOCK EXCHANGE

111 BROADWAY

TRINITY CHURCH

NEW YORK STOCK EXCHANGE

CHARGING BULL

STATEN ISLAND FERRY TERMINAL

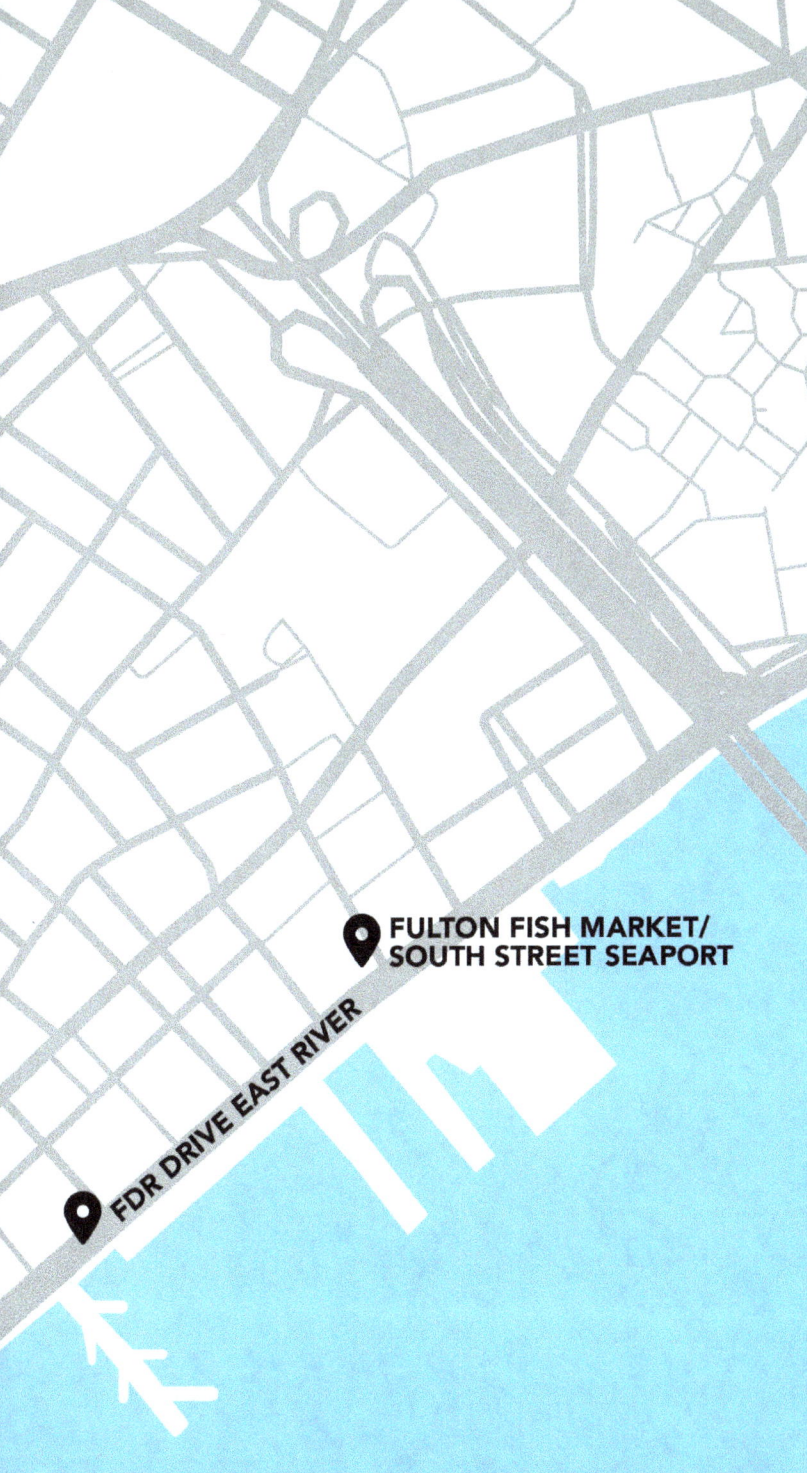

Chapter 4
STILL SOLDIER STRONG

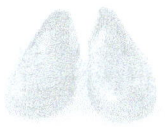

Our second daughter turned five on April 27, 2011. As happens with two young children in the house, it was a hectic day. It was also one of those wonderful spring days in Stamford that teases you with the idea that summer might be around the corner.

I can still remember the morning's frantic pace. I had to pick up an ice cream cake and balloons, while Christine was busy wrapping presents. Meanwhile, we hurried to get the house cleaned and ready for the party. Soon we'd be singing "Happy Birthday," and watching her rifle through her presents while her friends devoured slices of cake. We thought that *we* had our hands full. Perhaps we did. Still, our concerns pointed back to joy, and were centered around making the day special for our daughter.

Some 6,800 miles away, Army Sergeant Dan Rose was part of Operation Enduring Freedom in Afghanistan. Like all who volunteer to secure our freedoms, Sergeant Rose would experience a much different kind of day. He and his crew had spent months in Afghanistan hunting for, finding, and disarming the Taliban's improvised explosive devices (IEDs). About halfway through his patrol route, he came upon a culvert that had been filled in on both ends, making it impossible to tell that it was even still there. In fact, the Taliban had spent two months of the rainy season, when

US forces were not patrolling that particular road, to fill the culvert with a thousand pounds of explosives.

Dan's truck was directly above it when the explosion happened. It would cost him the use of his legs, and permanently paralyze him from the chest down.

Much to his credit, Sergeant Rose has no regrets about joining the military. In the Reserves through college, he actively chose deployment to Afghanistan when, during the financial crisis, the right job opportunity was hard to come by. He may have lost the ability to walk on his own, but his sense of humor remains. Years later, he still jokes that his squad had a 100% find ratio, "until we didn't," as he puts it.

Something he doesn't joke about is the fact that he considers the day of the explosion to be a "great day." How? Well, despite hitting the buried IED, Dan sustained the worst injuries of his crew. In fact, none of his crewmates sustained permanent injuries. I've been privileged to see this kind of attitude many times since meeting Dan, someone I consider to be a true hero.

Oddly enough, Dan was no stranger to severe injuries. He'd broken his back twice in his youth—once while playing hockey, the other time while riding a four-wheeler. His previous injuries bred a sense of confidence that would eventually work against him.

"I'd been through it," he thought. "This will be easy. I'll get surgery, then will be back at it."

After surgery at Walter Reed, he asked the surgeon how long before he could get up and out. The surgeon's reply was pointblank.

"You're never going to walk again."

The news crushed Dan, but also clarified things for him.

"In a way, it was a good thing to hear. I was able to get over the pipedream of walking, and focus on what I had to do to get out of the hospital."

Dan's next step was rehab at the VA medical center in Tampa, Florida. With the direct therapy department, he began to see that life wasn't going to be as bad as he thought.

"I knew I wouldn't be just sitting on the sidelines."

Still, like many other heroes from the front, Dan began to encounter challenges once he returned to his hometown. Every day, he would catch a glimpse of things he could no longer do. Bars and restaurants without ramps became off limits to him. He could no longer ski, which he had loved. The initial aftershocks of his new life back home began to unravel his identity.

Dan's experience is a reminder that for many wounded veterans, their sacrifices don't end once they leave the battlefield. In the vast majority of cases, they come home to a veterans system that runs in an old, one-size-fits-all manner.

Let me say this about our veterans system before I go forward: without a doubt, it is driven by the very best intentions. What's more, most Americans believe that the veterans of the best military in the world *should* have access to the best care in the world.

Today, "having access to the best care" means providing innovative, customized, and responsive solutions that aren't easy to come by in a system that still operates in an antiquated way.

At the end of 2013, roughly two and a half years after his injury, Dan and I met for the first time. By then, the US wars in Iraq and Afghanistan were winding down to a large degree—it would be almost another full decade before our last troops left Afghanistan.

As I learned more about Dan and his story, I began to understand how our support needed to shift in order to help a new group of service members take their next steps.

By now, SoldierSocks had successfully shipped more than 75,000 pounds of direct supplies to deployed military members. With the wars winding down, more and more troops were coming home. In other words, the need for socks and baby wipes was not the same as it had been in 2009.

Likewise, our smaller offshoot programs—things like sending *thank*-you notes, Valentine's Day cards, and holiday cheer—began to feel outmoded as well. Yes, we could have continued to ship supplies, but the idea of resting on our laurels and staying in our lane didn't feel right. We wanted to make as meaningful a contribution as possible, and to fill the biggest need we could.

Around this time, we considered shutting SoldierSocks down. Perhaps we *had* accomplished our mission, and our duty had run its course. Maybe it was time to close operations and declare victory. Fortunately, the idea of shutting down started to shift. Saying goodbye was one thing. What about evolving into something new?

Scott Duffy and I were discussing our work one night, and remembering our experiences on 9/11. We agreed that it was time to hash out our next steps. That's when he made an interesting point. "Well Chris," he said, "what happens to the ones who don't just need new socks, but who have been hit by some terrible IED? Imagine helping *them* take their next steps forward?"

Our conversation soon turned toward what we saw as a mentality of victimization when it came to caring for veterans. "We treat them as though they're victims," Scott said, with which I agreed. "They're not victims. They're some of the strongest people we've ever met. They may have lost some physical ability, but they are still *soldier strong*."

What an amazing expression and way to encapsulate the strength of body, mind, character, and spirit that marks every American serviceman and woman. That phrase was like a thunderclap, and it would stick with me in the days and weeks to come. Eventually, it became our new rallying cry—and our new name.

Fired up by this new charge, I quickly jumped into as much reading and research as I could. I wanted to learn about how our catastrophically injured soldiers were being treated upon their return. What I discovered was that the support they received was often riddled with major gaps and issues.

Thankfully, many of our soldiers were coming home to a hero's welcome—an important change from the return that many vets of the Vietnam era experienced. Once home, however, these same heroes soon found themselves carrying the label of "broken veterans" rather than "injured soldiers." Too often, well-intentioned charities were coddling them, unwittingly advancing the *veteran-as-victim* mentality.

Perhaps most alarmingly, at least from the vantage of receiving the best care possible, these vets also found themselves stuck trying to navigate a horribly outdated VA system, one still designed for a much different and earlier time. Despite the best intentions, the VA was struggling to meet 21st century problems, or provide next-gen care to this generation of veterans.

Let me offer an important note here, concerning the VA: I have had the esteemed privilege of working with several dozen VA hospitals and medical centers from around the country, interfacing directly with elite doctors, nurses, clinicians, and care providers in the process. Their compassion is without question. They work tirelessly for veterans. My criticisms of the VA are related to systemic challenges, but do not extend to the men and women who work on these medical frontlines.

I used the word *antiquated* earlier; it really is the best way to describe many of the systems and processes that still exist within the VA today, nearly a decade after Scott Duffy first uttered the phrase *soldier strong*. Here's a fact that literally shocked me when I first learned about it: while the VA builds a number of prosthetic arms, one of the primary prosthetic arms they give to upper limb amputees is based on early 20th century technology—literally patented in 1919!

That's right: many of today's injured veterans receive prosthetics that are not all that different from what veterans of the First World War received. Obviously, things have changed quite a bit since then—just go compare a Tesla and a Ford Model T. Shouldn't one of today's amputees receive something more advanced than they would have received had they fought in the Somme Defensive of 1918?

When you learn facts like these, it's like a slap to the face. It sinks in very quickly just how ill-equipped our old system is in the face of new challenges.

With our energy renewed, we began thinking of ways to expand our mission. We'd helped servicemen and women take next steps forward with socks and baby wipes. What could we do for veterans?

More than anything, we wanted to address the fact that veterans were not receiving the most modern tools to help them move forward in life. Between the Vietnam era and post-9/11 deployments, there had been some extraordinary developments in what we understood about battlefield injuries. One major study[4] from 2015 focused on the period of time known as the "golden hour"—the 60 minutes between a catastrophic battlefield injury, and permanent, irreversible damage or death.

The US Department of Defense, along with each branch of the military, had spent decades learning about, studying, and perfecting techniques to support injured soldiers in that golden hour. They had effectively been able to turn the tide on many grievous battlefield injuries that, even a generation earlier, may have proven fatal.

However, their success had created something of a paradoxical challenge: with more grievously wounded personnel surviving, the VA was having a difficult time supporting them with the levels of care they needed. Sadly, the military's golden hour commitment did not extend to delivering revolutionary treatments, devices, and recuperation support back home.

NEXT STEPS FORWARD

As time went on, the *still soldier strong* idea continued to stick with me. Every time I thought about our veterans, I grappled with what felt like a daunting, potentially life-defining question: How could our little charity from Stamford, Connecticut—one that shipped tube socks and baby wipes—help fix this problem? I kept circling back to a word that had meant so much to me since my early days in finance: innovation.

I've always believed in America's culture of innovation and creativity. True, the Model T may not stack up that well against a modern Tesla, but it certainly was much more than *a faster horse* when it first arrived. The idea of American innovation is what attracted me to working in the financial sector. Every day, I found myself on the cusp of something new, an insider's look into what was there, and what was coming next. Here I was again, on the hunt for innovation—this time, I wanted to find the most innovative way possible to expand our mission, and help veterans take their next steps.

First, we revisited our own scholarship program, which we'd launched a year earlier, to help fill the post-9/11 GI Bill gap. We quickly established two new programs for veterans who wanted to explore careers in public service. The first scholarship was connected with the top public policy school in the country, the Maxwell School at Syracuse University. The second was at the nation's top foreign-service school, the Walsh School at Georgetown University. Later, we generated a new program for female veterans who want to pursue STEM-focused degrees at Old Dominion University in Virginia.

Many wonderful students have benefited from these programs. Two of our earliest recipients were Jesse Campion and Toni Rico.

Jesse lost his father while he was getting his MPA at Syracuse. During that time, he stepped up to take care of his brother, while completing his studies. Later, he went on to earn his JD and LLM from Georgetown University, and has built an exciting career in national defense, law and policy.

Toni was our first Georgetown scholarship recipient. Since graduating, she's built a 10-plus year career in strategic communications and journalism, including reporting from combat zones.

Today, we're committed to making sure that other veterans continue to benefit from this program. With that said, even when we first launched the scholarships, the energy felt like we were just warming up. What about a veteran like Dan Rose? Was a scholarship what he needed most? What would help him and other veterans in similar situations move past the physical aftershocks of their service?

Scott and I believed that we owed it to Dan, and to hundreds of veterans like him, to keep up our end of the bargain—to truly go all-in on finding and delivering the best technology and opportunities we could. The innovation was out there. We needed to bring it forward.

One of our board members discovered California-based Ekso Bionics. Their innovative exoskeleton suit enabled paralyzed people to do what was once unthinkable—stand and walk.[5] It was a perfect fit for our mission, and a chance to actually help veterans take literal next steps forward.

Without any relationship or introduction, I simply reached out to the company's CEO on LinkedIn. I told him I was going to be in San Francisco a few weeks later on business, and asked if I could stop by their facility. His reply came back pretty quickly—Yes.

When I finally toured Ekso Bionics, I couldn't help but think about the James Bond franchise—legs and robots were moving around everywhere, and the whole place reminded me of where 007 secures the latest and greatest in spy tech. Before I left the building, I committed to funding ten Ekso Suits. There was a catch, of course: each suit cost $150k. Our small organization had never raised $150,000 in a single year, let alone a multiple of ten! To raise $1.5 million would require some significant steps.

Here's something that the murderers who brought terrorism to our shores don't understand about American culture: we are made differently. It's true. We value the breathtaking awe of watching miracles happen through the confluence of will, support, sacrifice, and innovation. We cherish the knowledge of what Sergeant Rose and many others like him gave up for us, and the dedication of scientists, doctors, caregivers and technologists to help bring that ability back to him.

In the days and months after my first tour of Ekso Bionics, our organization made a concerted effort to attract bigger levels of support. One of the most instrumental connections I've ever made is with Craig Pintoff, an executive at United Rentals, the world's largest equipment rental company—which happens to be headquartered in Stamford. We met in 2014, and he shared his goal of making sure United Rentals led the way when it came to hiring veterans. Craig quickly committed $25,000 to our organization via their foundation, opened the door to future engagements, and has continued to support our work.

A year later, we participated in the NFL's Salute to Service program, which featured a veteran in one of our Soldier-Suits on the field during games in seven stadiums around the country. United Rentals contributed $50,000 that year in support of our Salute to Service programming. It was an excellent introduction to the cultural power of professional sports, and a strong reminder that our veterans had tens of thousands of fans and supporters who would wildly cheer them on.

In 2016, United Rentals added Chris Hummel as their Chief Marketing Officer. I met Chris over lunch one day in Stamford. He had decided that United Rentals would sponsor an IndyCar team co-owned by racing legend Bobby Rahal, iconic comedian and talk show host David Letterman, and businessman Mike Lanigan.

On top of sponsoring the team, Hummel proposed continued support for our organization via a new program he named Turns for Troops. United Rentals committed to donate $50 to Turns for Troops for every lap the IndyCar team completed during the season. In 2016, the program generated $134,000 for our organization.

That season I had the good fortune to meet Graham Rahal, the team's star driver, at the Grand Prix of Sonoma. Not only had he taken all of those laps, but he had a real and meaningful personal interest in our veterans. We awarded Graham our annual Commitment to Service Award during our 2016 gala.

David Letterman, so well-known for his sharp wit, was an extraordinary supporter. A paralyzed veteran attended each Indy 500 race between 2017 and 2019, and Letterman, who is one of the most sought after celebrities in America, could not have been kinder, more accessible, or more gracious to them. Every time I saw him, I quickly remembered his immensely moving and personal post-9/11 monologue, where he spoke of the American character. He had true compassion for those who served, and especially showed it in private settings when nobody was watching.

By 2019, the Graham and Courtney Rahal Foundation added more support for our programming. We became a primary beneficiary of their Drive for a Cause golf tournament, which raised a combined $380,000 between 2019 and 2021. In 2021, Graham and Courtney launched Vino for Vets, which raised an additional $150,000 for our more recent work in mental health care.

In total, as of the end of 2021, United Rentals has raised roughly $1.4 million on our behalf through their programs, while the Graham and Courtney Rahal Foundation has added more than $530,000 to our cause. Such extraordinary partners have empowered a great deal of the innovation we have been able to identify and fund.

No matter how far our organization has gone and grown, I'm not sure how much of it would have happened without Sergeant Dan Rose. When we finally met in person in December 2013, not long after my initial commitment to the Ekso Suit, it was the honor of my lifetime to make him our very first SoldierSuit recipient. The suits themselves were so advanced, it was easy to get swept up into thinking that they belonged in a sci-fi movie. As soon as I saw Dan stand up from his wheelchair and walk around the room, I came back to reality in a very powerful way.

Why did it matter, and why does it still matter? In part, because everyone involved in the chain refused to believe that Dan had lost his ability to walk for good. His first steps since his injury may have been a culmination of sorts, but we had a very long way to go. I'm proud to say that since this first Ekso Suit, we have donated 24 more to VA medical centers, veteran rehabilitation facilities, and individual veterans all around the country.

One of the essential pivots we started to make in 2013, and have continued to make, is to provide devices to VA medical centers instead of individual veterans. There are a few reasons. First, the technology isn't quite ready. They're not made for people to wear for 12 to 15 hours a day. They work better as rehabilitative devices, and VA centers make ideal locations for this type of support.

Secondly, we learned we are not fully equipped to choose which veterans will or will not receive an exoskeleton, and enjoy the ability to walk again. When we went through our first selection process, we were literally *playing God* by determining who would be able to stand and look the world in the eye once more. It wasn't our place, especially when you consider that more than 300,000 US veterans live with spinal cord injuries, and the number continues to grow.

Thankfully, we discovered that we don't have to pinpoint one specific serviceman or woman to receive a suit. These devices easily adjust to fit multiple people. In one way of thinking, they work just like gym equipment, made to support one person for a short amount of time, then support someone new in steady rotation.

Little more than a year after Sergeant Dan Rose stepped forward with the help of an Ekso Suit, amidst the funding support I mentioned above, we decided it was time to don a new organizational name and banner. SoldierSocks was our beginning, and SoldierSuits served to propel us forward, but the name we chose went back to that critical conversation Scott Duffy and I had in the spring of 2013: we were now SoldierStrong. The new name echoed Scott's words, and reflected our evolution.

We were no longer just about sending tube socks and baby wipes to forward deployed troops. We were here to help service members—active and veterans—take their next steps forward. Even when their bodies suffered life-altering injuries, their spirits, courage, or mental fortitude remained intact. In many cases, they actually grew stronger. They were the ones who were truly soldier strong. Our work was about them.

Chapter 5

DARPA FOR WOUNDS OF WAR

The transformation from SoldierSocks to SoldierStrong proved to be a radical shift. In the first few months after the name change, I began to feel more at home with our mission's new focus.

Since the early days of my professional life, I had invested in transformational brands and revolutionary products—that word *innovation* again. SoldierSocks had certainly filled an important and immediate need: in the parlance of my trading career, we had "supplied an unmet demand in an important market niche." Yes, the work felt good, and had made a difference. However, it had always been a "market-driven" response, and not exactly a transformational or revolutionary idea.

SoldierStrong was a serious shift that went head-on toward solving a larger set of problems. With the Ekso device, we'd moved *way beyond* tube socks and baby wipes. Now, we were creating a foundation that could potentially help every paralyzed veteran recoup physical capabilities that many believed they had lost forever.

I had no interest in just giving paralyzed veterans *a better wheelchair*—it would have been the same as Ford creating a faster horse. I wanted our brave men and women to stand up and take literal and actionable next steps forward. Someone else could focus on evolutionary changes—we wanted *revolutionary* advancements for our veterans.

The pattern of innovation that soon emerged always pointed back to a common starting point: we pursued ways to formalize and expand our model in order to provide true, next-gen advancements. We started with the Ekso device, and soon explored others. The result was something we called the SoldierSuit. Each suit included components from different manufacturers, and the combined effect was profound.

Among the companies and organizations we turned to included Parker Hannifin, Myomo, Bionx, DEKA Research, and Mobius Mobility. Walking into Ekso Bionics' facility had been like entering a James Bond movie, but now we were truly in the thick of it. Many of the devices that caught our interest were byproducts of US military research. We valued these American-made innovations, and saw them as the absolute best options for American heroes.

Myomo leads the way in extending myoelectric prosthetic technology to powered braces. These help restore function for people with neuromuscular conditions. In essence, they give veterans with certain injuries new ways to support and move their arms again. With Myomo, we delivered the MyoPro to veterans with upper extremity impairment after traumatic brain or spinal cord injuries, and other neurological disabilities.

Bionx produces bionic solutions that help amputees regain normalized functions. Through them we provided the BiOM ankle, the market's only powered propulsion prosthesis.

It offers more power, stability, and control than any other lower extremity prosthetic.

DEKA Research has also been a revolutionary partner for us. With their prosthetic, wearers can use and move their arm, wrist, and hand in ways that truly mimic how the human arm functions in the world. We have proudly been providing these arms to veterans since 2015.

As I delved deeper and deeper into tracking down the most revolutionary devices and partners, I kept bumping into the Defense Advanced Research Projects Agency—DARPA. Initially, I possessed only a passing familiarity with them. I knew I needed to learn more.

Exploring the DARPA Model

One major issue our veterans face, which became clearer as I assessed the VA's attempts to improve performance, is that the VA is appropriately in the service-delivery business. Even major, VA-related policy proposals cap out at improving the agency's service delivery. In a nutshell, they exist to support and serve as best they can, but are not built to innovate.

To some extent, certain proposals do foster or accelerate innovation, but only in the policy sense—not in terms of medical or scientific advancements. As important as policy innovation is, it is no substitute for real-life scientific and medical innovation.

The business of innovating on a revolutionary scale takes a different mindset, skillset, and structure than service delivery. Per current policy, the VA treats veterans like any other medical population, regardless of their specialized, individual needs. This approach relies on decades-long research into and developing new treatments and technologies—mainly for private market success. Since the special nature of service-related medical issues limits market size, this approach does not serve members of our veteran population.

Within the federal government, this problem is not unique. The Department of Defense regularly needs technical tools that the private marketplace would not (or could not) develop. However, DARPA is the DoD's solution to addressing this issue.

With an annual budget of approximately $3.44 billion, DARPA is responsible for imagining the battlefield of the future, and creating technologies to combat future needs and situations. The agency has a solid track record of scientific innovation. The internet is a result of DARPA, as is GPS, plus hundreds of other technologies that have made their way into our lives—and that will continue to do so in the future.

DARPA officially spends its budget to "formulate and execute research and development projects to extend the frontiers of technology and science, with the aim to reach beyond immediate military requirements." Their mission is "to prevent technological surprise to the US, but also to create technological surprise for our enemies."

In recent years, DARPA has undertaken at least two major programs that aim to replace or supplement human performance factors: the robotic exoskeleton (designed to allow ground forces to wear and/or carry hundreds of pounds of additional equipment and body armor), and a robotic arm (designed to mimic the full range of motion of the human arm from the shoulder through the fingertips, in order to keep bomb technicians a safe distance from devices they must disarm).

Byproducts of these programs make exceptional medical devices. The exoskeleton allows paralyzed veterans to stand and walk again, and allows stroke victims to safely regain muscle movement and strength. The bionic arm is the first prosthetic that replaces the full range of motion for amputees, and has the potential to be "plugged in" to the central nervous system, which would allow recipients to control their arm by thinking about it.

If these advances sound familiar, you're onto something. These "byproducts" are exactly what SoldierStrong began identifying and delivering to the VA. Yet, SoldierStrong began doing so not through a formal arrangement, but after a relentless search for the best, most innovative technologies we could find to fill the critical needs of veterans.

The reason it took a charitable organization like SoldierStrong is simple: DARPA is prohibited by federal law from working on projects that are not directly defense-oriented. This is a relic of Cold War-era policymaking that looked to constrain the reach of the military industrial complex.

However, as I mentioned earlier, more and more of today's servicemen and women are surviving grievous injuries that would have been fatal in earlier conflicts—the result of the golden hour focus. The unintended result is that, at a time when more veterans than ever need hyper-advanced medical devices, the preeminent research operation that could be addressing their unique needs is handcuffed from doing so.

America's servicemen and women have access to the best, most advanced technological tools our government can create, thanks to a dedicated agency that imagines the battlefield of the future, and invents responsive technologies today. SoldierStrong believes that America's paralyzed veterans should benefit from a similar commitment after their injuries. Where is the DARPA-like agency that's dedicated to their needs?

Creating, embracing, and accelerating innovation will not happen by focusing on policy proposals that seek to create a more efficient delivery service. While solving service delivery challenges is laudable and imperative, it's simply not enough.

America's veterans, especially those who sacrificed physical ability in defense of our liberties, should expect the same level of technological commitment we provide front line service members. The needs of this community are much different than those we find in the private marketplace—to meet them would require a VA-backed arrangement to lead technical development. I believe that the VA would be smart to replicate the successful DARPA model.

Working from this belief, our mission at SoldierStrong has become, in part, to facilitate this approach more rapidly than American policymakers are able or willing to do from a policy platform. The limitation for SoldierStrong, however, is that we operate as an outside charity, rather than a partner from within DARPA, DoD, or the VA. Therefore, we must seek out and find innovations on our own. Still, we fundamentally believe that if a small, lean organization like ours can "stumble into" several DARPA-funded byproducts that have the potential for revolutionary improvement in the lives of veterans, a formal avenue for a federal commitment to innovation would be even more fruitful.

"VARPA" or Veterans Advanced Research Projects Agency

A veteran-focused version of DARPA, "VARPA" (as we'll call it here) could focus on a variety of tech transfer initiatives, such as those outlined above, from DARPA to the veterans space. This future-minded organization could also play a critical connecting role between the VA and the NIH Brain-Mapping project, the objective of which is to map the functioning of the human brain the way we mapped the functioning of the human genome over the last two decades.

This approach would provide a formal structure that's committed to innovation, and let the VA stay focused on service delivery. This would dramatically expand options to veterans who have survived grievous injuries.

Here's an important issue to bring up again, which I noted earlier: the underlying technology in prosthetic arms that the VA offers for free to most upper-extremity amputees was patented in the World War I era. Now, here's something I'd like to add to this critical point: while the VA has conducted cost analysis on acquiring newer technologies, they have never adequately studied veteran experience.

Think about that for a moment. How much different would post-injury life be for veterans who have access to newer prosthetic technologies—solutions that allow them to control their limbs with their own central nervous system, for instance, modulate grip strength, and even receive tactile feedback through sensors in the prosthetic?

These types of advancements replicate themselves over a wide variety of medical conditions and technical products. This range moves quickly from prosthetics, which are currently available from existing DARPA projects, to brain health issues, including traumatic brain injury (TBI), PTSD, and even addiction.

Filling the Gap

I suspect that the vast majority of Americans are proud of the fact that we have the strongest military in the history of the world—not to mention the most technologically advanced. We spare no effort or expense to equip our warfighters with the best technologies, and tools we can conceive of—as well we should.

Where does this leave our veterans? What about those who have sacrificed physical ability in the service of our country? Don't they deserve the same commitment? I believe they do—and I bet that most people reading this book believe the same.

For so many of us, the wars that started in the aftermath of 9/11 have ended. However, they *haven't* ended for those who sacrificed various physical abilities in the process of defending our country. Since 9/11 alone, our men and women in uniform have encountered more than 52,000 combat related injuries—and this number doesn't include an estimated 320,000 TBI, or 400,000 PTSD cases.

The VA is there for them, and we're privileged to work with wonderful and committed professionals who care deeply about our vets. Still, we believe, as do many within the VA, that their organization is confined by a bureaucratic set of outdated rules that can't keep up with the pace of innovation our economy is built to produce.

Beyond any shadow of a doubt, members of the best military in the world should have access to the greatest care imaginable when they come home. Today, that means innovative, customized, responsive solutions that the old system cannot provide. It means creating and following through on the level of commitment to veterans that DARPA offers to warfighters.

Why is there no DARPA for veterans? Why does the VA system continue to deliver solutions that pair with grossly outdated technology? This does not pass the test of what America is about at our core. Nor does it meet our collective obligation and duty to maintain our commitment to soldiers long after the battle is done.

SoldierStrong is doing our best to fill the gap, and the work can feel terribly isolating at times. Case in point: of the more than 46,000 military and veteran focused non-profits in the country, SoldierStrong is the only one focused specifically on delivering revolutionary medical devices, many of which come from DARPA research.

Here's a question I cannot stop asking: once battlefield science is done, why is there no more funding to push developments into non-military applications for veterans? Many of these technologies seem to have come straight out of the future—a fact that points to DARPA living up to its mission. They help people do things that may have once been impossible. Just imagine what more we could accomplish if we were willing, able, and equipped to push past the roadblocks that hold innovation at bay.

What would it take to replace the wheelchair not with *a better wheelchair*, but with new legs? What would it mean for amputees to receive a new arm that functions just like the original? What type of user experience data would such profound developments produce?

NEXT STEPS FORWARD

If you're like me, then being able to see these things through is a source of excitement and inspiration. This is what the next generation looks like—or could look like. It's what honoring our commitment to our veterans should look like. It's what's waiting on the other side of every closed door—if we are willing to open them.

Chapter 6
FIGHTING INVISIBLE WOUNDS

Did you know that 22 American veterans take their lives every day in our country? That estimate adds up to 8,030 veteran suicides per year. To put that number into perspective, that's more than the population of places such as Aspen, Colo., Rockport, Mass., Moab, Utah, Bar Harbor, Maine, and hundreds of other areas throughout the country. Yes—we lose a town's worth of veterans every year to suicide.

Suicide is always tragic, but it seems especially so for veterans. Their suicides often directly relate to their service. Consider: the suicide rate among veterans is significantly higher than that of the general population; and, as modern medicine learns more about brain health, it's becoming clear that the invisible wounds of war are the driving factors behind suicide ideation and attempts.[6]

What are the invisible wounds of war? They include things like PTSD, ringing in the ears, TBI, chronic traumatic encephalopathy (CTE), and many more challenges that veterans face every day. Brain science may be a fairly new discipline, but these wounds of war have been around for centuries. As far back as 500 B.C., we have recorded reports of what we now know as PTSD. Herodotus refers to "tremblers," and Pantites, the Spartan warrior who founded the now famous "300" after the Battle of Thermopylae, hanged himself after being shunned as one.

NEXT STEPS FORWARD

Our medical understanding of the long-term impacts and ongoing effects from service-related brain injuries has only recently come into focus. Still, despite advances in brain science and medical understanding, the consequences for veterans are not new. For some context, consider that there are 58,282 names on the Vietnam Memorial Wall in Washington, D.C.; however, more Vietnam-era veterans have been lost to suicide in the years *since* the war ended than are listed on that wall. Many of today's post-9/11 veterans find themselves on the same trajectory.

Thankfully, in the last few years, science has opened new doors into understanding the invisible wounds of war, and American innovation is starting to catch up. SoldierStrong's model of identifying and deploying revolutionary advancements to address physical wounds of war is the exact model we need to make true progress in addressing the invisible wounds as well.

Our organization's journey into brain health started on January 20, 2016. I was at the Denver VA Medical Center to donate a SoldierSuit. Dr. Lisa Brenner, the director of the Rocky Mountain VA, told me that in addition to using the device for physical rehabilitation, they were also going to use it as part of a mental health study. She explained that the study would look at the mental health benefits of being able to stand up and, to paraphrase, "see the world at eye level again."

The clinicians at the Denver VA were onto something very important and exciting. They were exploring the integrated nature of physical and emotional health in real time, and the results of their initial study were outstanding.

The mental and psychological health of their veteran population improved dramatically with even limited regular use of the SoldierSuit. In addition, harmful thoughts and suicide ideation decreased. When I saw the preliminary results, it made immediate sense. By then, I'd been around many veterans who'd suffered serious spinal cord injuries, and had learned from these men and women just how powerful the ability to stand and walk again can be. Dr. Brenner and other professionals at the Denver VA were proving out what we'd been suspecting: the visible wounds of war also have an invisible component; as physical wellbeing improves, so does psychological health.

Many people focus on a device's technical components: how something works, why it works, how a tweak here or there can make it work better, etc. However, the actual user experience is always more visceral than cerebral.

Even veterans with complete spinal injuries and irreversible paralysis experience many physical benefits when they use the SoldierSuit: better flexibility, improved skin health, better digestive functioning, and an increased ability to stand and walk in the future are a few that come to mind. However, the psychological and emotional responses from real-world use are even more powerful.

Most veterans aren't shy about expressing these benefits directly. They speak of how good it feels to see the world at eye level again, and to stand upright among peers—rather than constantly having to look up. Some of their experiences are even more poignant: being able to stand eye-to-eye with their partners on their wedding days, or to walk their daughters down the aisle are truly transformative moments for soldiers who thought they'd never walk again.

NEXT STEPS FORWARD

Former Army National Guard Sergeant First Class Matt Ross is from Charles City, Iowa. Following his deployments, Sergeant Ross was involved in a farm accident that left him with a broken back between his shoulder blades.

"I spent seven hours in surgery that night," Sergeant Ross shared with me when we met. "I died three times on the table, the last time for half an hour. I've actually gotten to meet the doctor who massaged my heart to keep me alive."

After surgery, the doctors told Sergeant Ross's family that he'd never walk again, and to adapt the house for a wheelchair. However, that wasn't the end of Ross's story—in fact, a new journey was just about to start. The Minneapolis VA reached out to let him know that they had just received their first Ekso Suit. Just 10 weeks after the date of his accident, he stood up out of his wheelchair and walked 15 feet.

From there, Sergeant Ross was determined to keep proving his surgeons wrong, and continued regular Ekso Suit therapy sessions. As time went on, he had a new target in mind: to walk his daughter down the aisle on her wedding day.

In a later conversation, his own words conveyed his profound joy. "Within 18 months, I went from hearing that I would never walk again, to standing and walking on my own, to eventually doing the father-daughter dance at my daughter's wedding."

Such experiences and memories heal more than the body's visible wounds of war. They heal the mind, and give people something for which to hope, fight, and strive.

Fighting Invisible Wounds

When the Denver VA began to capture and quantify these results, I knew they were right on track, and it lit a fire under our own efforts to do even more for veterans. By now, we had supported deployed personnel through SoldierSocks, and had addressed visible wounds of war with Soldier-Strong and the SoldierSuit. It was time to pivot again, and apply our model of innovation and action toward healing the invisible wounds of war.

We knew there was a lot of work to do when it came to addressing brain health. We went full steam ahead into learning from and listening to experts, researching problems, needs, and issues, and identifying as many cutting-edge solutions as possible. One topic we zeroed in on was the fact that the most common underlying factor for veterans who consider or attempt suicide is un-remediated post-traumatic stress.

A recent RAND corporation analysis found that 2,770,000 American service members have served some 5,400,000 deployments since the 9/11 terror attacks.[7] Those deployments have created a significant number of relatively young veterans who face disproportionate rates of mental health issues as a consequence of their service.

This same RAND analysis, which includes research findings from the National Institutes of Health (NIH), found the prevalence of mental health issues increases significantly after a deployment. It also found that PTSD and depression were the two leading forms of mental health issues returning service members face.

As I mentioned at the start of this chapter, 22 US military veterans commit suicide every day. The VA continues to study the connection between PTSD and veteran suicides, but the statistical link stands out: when compared to multiple anxiety diagnoses, PTSD is significantly associated with suicidal ideation, and suicide attempts among veterans.

The VA has been focusing on PTSD since before the end of the Cold War—the agency founded its National Center for PTSD in 1989. Their stated goal at the time was to improve care and education through research into prevention, causes, assessment, and treatment of traumatic stress disorders. Sadly, more than 30 years later, the rate of veteran suicide remains shockingly high, and the relationship between PTSD and veteran suicide is a clear indication that critical, persistent gaps in care remain.

Is the VA failing our veterans? No, I do not believe so. However, I believe that the size, scale, and complexity of this situation require a revolutionary reconsideration of how best to combat the mental health issues our veterans face. In fact, I believe, as do my partners in this fight, that addressing this crisis is a national responsibility.

The VA maintains a world-class program for PTSD; however, progress has been too slow, and we continue to lose 22 veterans to suicide every day. Delving deeper, it's important to keep in mind that PTSD is just one of many mental health challenges our veterans and their families face.

While suicidal ideation and suicide attempts are the most extreme expression of mental health issues, they are not the only ones, or even the most common. For example:

- Estimates suggest that more than 1.75 million, post-9/11 veterans have suffered TBI. This affliction is so prevalent that it has earned the unfortunate title of "the signature wound" of Operation Enduring Freedom and Operation Iraqi Freedom.

- Recent data shows that more than 30% of veterans have been diagnosed with a mental health disorder, and 40% have been diagnosed with a mental health or behavioral adjustment disorder. However, due to social and societal stigma around such diagnoses, the number of cases may under-represent the actual incidence of such conditions.

- Concerning the spouses of veterans, 20% are in some form of counseling for related issues.

- Post-deployment, 15% of US military personnel turn to opioid use, compared to just 4% of the total US population.

- Alarmingly, recent projections suggest that the trends listed above will worsen in coming years.

Thankfully, medical science has begun addressing the fact that our understanding of how the brain functions isn't nearly as robust as our understanding of how the body works. As I mentioned in chapter 5, the NIH has embarked on a project to map the functioning of the human brain, modeling their approach on the human genome mapping project of the last two decades. The hope is that their work will become the foundation for future research into solving vexing brain and mental health conditions.

Meanwhile, the Veterans Administration continues to grapple mightily with these issues, and policy makers have made several attempts to address them as well. This includes legislative and executive branch actions, formal studies, policy changes, and new appropriations. Still, our veterans struggle every day with mental health care issues, challenges, and concerns.

We began to conclude that even though the VA was trying, its massive scale, along with a bureaucratic service delivery model, were conspiring to keep radical innovation at bay. Once again, the lack of a DARPA-like service capability for veterans (our "VARPA" concept from chapter 5) was painfully obvious.

Without VARPA, SoldierStrong took it upon ourselves to fill as much of the gap as any small charitable organization can do. We shifted our focus, and began to apply our model of speeding the deployment of revolutionary technological advancements to those who needed them.

With so many possibilities in the brain health space, we decided to zero in on issues that presented as serious and durable problems, but with which our model could have clear success.

While preventing suicide is only one of many outcomes of promoting brain health, the suicide rate among veterans was an important and measurable place to start. And, having learned that PTSD was a leading underlying factor in veteran suicide ideation and attempts, we began looking for cutting-edge PTSD treatments. That search led us to BraveMind.

Chapter 7

BRAVEMIND

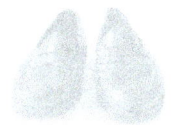

The search for technical innovations to address brain health, maximize brain performance, and mitigate brain injuries began as many modern searches do: by typing key words and phrases into Google.

We knew we had a model that had worked for visible wounds of war: identify, fund, and expedite the delivery of revolutionary technology to those whose lives have been most impacted by their service to our nation. We also knew that PTSD was a leading common factor for veterans who had suicide ideation, or had attempted suicide. Yet, we knew precious little else about where to start.

In searching for the technical cutting edge, we wanted to find a tool or set of tools that fit our model of making revolutionary gains in capability, but had not yet emerged fully into the clinical world. At the start, we met with some disappointments: half-baked ideas, well-intentioned but unproven approaches, and as much myth and fiction as science and innovation. The early days and months of our search were frustrating, and sometimes reminded me of old *cure-all* remedies sold by slick, unscrupulous charmers on the Wild West frontier.

At one point, we reached out to a well-known mental health advocacy group to seek insights and advice. They could tell us plenty about what they perceived as being wrong with national and state public policy in various parts of the country. However, they were completely unprepared to prescribe innovations worth investing time and energy in—nor could they help identify potential breakthrough innovations in this space.

As our search progressed, we learned that some leading researchers had been awarded a Department of Defense investment to build virtual reality (VR) treatment capability that was highly promising for PTSD.

Perhaps counterintuitive for non-medical practitioners, the classical treatment for PTSD is known as immersion therapy. That is, rather than avoid the underlying cause, clinicians will actually take a patient back into the moment of the trauma, and work through the brain health issues that impact the experience. VR dramatically accelerates that process. Rather than a clinician having to talk a patient back into the setting or moment, VR allows a clinician to rapidly re-establish visual, audible, motion, and even scent cues from the original event or events.

We came across the work of Dr. Albert "Skip" Rizzo, who has become a pioneer, leading researcher, and something of an evangelist on the potential power of VR and VR Exposure Therapy (VRET) to heal in a clinical setting.

Rizzo is the director of medical virtual reality at the University of Southern California's Institute for Creative Technologies (ICT). He created Full Spectrum Warrior in 2004, an initial prototype of VR treatment for PTSD. Since then, the original system has gone through two evolutions (2006-2009 and 2010-2013), and received funding to create and test a version focused on military sexual trauma (MST).

To date, clinicians and patients in more than 100 sites have used the system, which continues to generate favorable clinical trial results as an evidence-based approach for delivering exposure therapy for combat and sexual trauma-related PTSD. At each phase of development, Rizzo and his team continue to improve the system, and concurrent evaluations of its effectiveness remain positive. In fact, the results have been so promising that the DoD funded the development of software, hardware, and a clinical study totaling some $30 million.

Yet, when we first discovered Rizzo's work, we found that the veterans community at large (at least as represented by the VA) did not have access to this tool set. In most cases, leading clinical service providers didn't even know it existed.

Dr. Rizzo was a continent away from my home in Connecticut. He and I had no mutual connections on LinkedIn, no known tie that I could leverage for an introduction. I went into internet sleuth mode and found his contact information after some searching, then sent him an email out of the blue. He must have thought I was crazy. In fact, he never responded to my first message, so I reached out a second time. I explained what SoldierStrong was all about, shared my background, and told him that we wanted to learn about and even support his work. When he finally responded in early 2019, he invited me to meet him at USC.

If you know the difference between winter in Stamford, Connecticut, versus Southern California, then it's no surprise that I accepted his invitation immediately. A small team of us flew to USC in February, for what would be the beginning of a partnership and friendship that is mutually dedicated to reducing the scourge of veteran suicide—and much more.

NEXT STEPS FORWARD

Dr. Rizzo—Skip to anyone who gets to know him—gave us the entire day. He brought his science team in, and carefully explained what they were doing, what they'd learned, what they thought they had, and—in a display of his integrity and transparency—what they *did not* have. Skip took us through his facility and demonstrated each component they were working on. He clearly had a command of the issues: the high-level medical research, clinical realities, details of the software, and the nuances of various pieces of hardware. He even had homemade prototypes of various ideas he had built to save costs and keep development going forward despite budget constraints.

Skip explained that many veterans and active service members are haunted by memories of specific disturbing events that occurred during combat. Oftentimes, they avoid such memories, and anything that triggers them, at any cost. That avoidance takes a heavy toll over time.

"They walk around angry all the time," he told us. "They don't want to talk to anyone about it. They don't want to even admit they have a problem."

Exposure therapy involves using the imagination to recall a troubling event, and talking through it with a therapist—it's a proven PTSD treatment strategy. However, veterans, especially those with depression in addition to PTSD, often find it difficult to willingly summon those memories. VR therapy changes the equation.

BraveMind's VR software includes 14 different "worlds," including settings such as a crowded Iraqi marketplace, a remote Afghan village, a checkpoint in the desert, and an operating base in the mountains. The therapist can recreate the scene of a traumatic incident in the VR headset, putting the veteran back in the moment.

Reliving your worst nightmare isn't easy. Dr. Rizzo calls virtual reality exposure therapy "hard medicine for a hard problem." Doing it in a safe, supportive environment, however, can help people open up about the incident, and process their emotions around it.

"It gets them talking about things they've never talked about before," said Dr. Rizzo. In the end, he said, "those memories don't have the same intense, painful, emotional power that they once did. Patients start to feel empowered, to feel that they got it out, and that they can talk about it."

For a veteran with PTSD, everyday civilian life can be fraught. Spotting a person dressed in Middle Eastern garb at a store or restaurant can generate a fight-or-flight response. Even just driving in traffic can be especially charged for vets. Garbage by the side of the road can trigger memories of an IED. Traveling through an underpass may bring back memories of a sniper on a bridge.

"You're always looking for the next shoe to drop," said Dr. Rizzo. "That might have been a survival skill in combat, but it doesn't work so well in civilian life."

Living on edge can strain relationships. "Sometimes, people with PTSD are difficult to be around," Dr. Rizzo shared. "That's when friends start falling away, or when vets get divorced." PTSD can alter a person's relationship with their children, too. A veteran who saw a young civilian killed in combat may not be able to dismiss the memory upon seeing his or her own child.

VR exposure therapy can gradually make difficult memories less harrowing, and help veterans with PTSD tamp down or even shut off the fight-or-flight mode. This allows them to take part in civilian life in more meaningful ways.

Our team was thoroughly impressed. Before we left that day, we discussed what Skip needed to get this technology and the promise of this treatment into the hands of VA clinicians, especially those on the front lines of the PTSD epidemic. Skip explained that, despite $30 million in federal investment, he didn't have a product for the VA. The reason was simple: the funding had been for a product that pre-treated soldiers who were about to deploy, in an attempt to reduce the incidence of PTSD in the first place.

I asked what he needed to finish converting the software for clinical veteran use. Then I tensed nearly every muscle in my body anticipating a stratospheric number. Skip replied, "Let me put some numbers together and get back to you."

In the meantime, he suggested that I go to the University of Texas at Dallas to visit their Center for BrainHealth. The center was doing some of the best work in the country on the clinical interface with improving brain performance and brain health outcomes.

UT-Dallas's Center for BrainHealth

I met Dr. Sandi Chapman not long after our visit to USC, at UT-Dallas's Center for BrainHealth. Sandi is a focused and driven evangelist for the idea that a revolution in brain health is coming. She's smart and persuasive, and runs an extraordinary research center that's focused on improving the brain performance of every American.

By focusing on health and performance, as opposed to a more traditional focus on addressing mental health issues and problems, Dr. Chapman and her team hope to revolutionize the way our culture thinks about and embraces brain health. I believe hers is one of the most important approaches to begin removing the stigma associated with brain health conditions and treatments, and help migrate the culture toward acceptance of brain health as an integral part of overall human wellbeing.

During our meeting, Dr. Chapman made a persuasive case that we have a proven, recent model of changing cultural attitudes about health. She rightly observed that in the 1940s and 1950s, a time when the American lifespan was significantly shorter than it is today, most citizens did not fully realize the impacts of diet, rest, and exercise on long-term wellness and health. As new science became accessible and understood, the public began to embrace healthier lifestyle choices. Today, for instance, it's no longer culturally acceptable to smoke inside, drive drunk, or eat only high-fat calories. In fact, we live at a time when more Americans have some form of health supplement and exercise regimen than ever before.

As Dr. Chapman explained, when Americans are armed with new knowledge about how brain health works, and the types of choices and activities that will improve brain performance, we will see a similarly significant change in behaviors and attitudes. More and more people will embrace brain-healthy habits, and begin to seek help when they need to do so—without fearing the stigma that's currently associated with brain health.

Dr. Chapman's program at UT-Dallas has helped advance scientific and clinical approaches to answering questions related to improving brain health and performance. In addition, the measurement and assessment tools her team has developed, alongside advice, guidance, and training tools for improving brain performance, are helping set a new standard in this space. Her progress has been so promising that the US Southern Command (SOCOM) sends special forces operators through her program for improved brain performance—no different than sending them through physical training to improve physical performance.

Dr. Chapman and her UT-Dallas team would become key clinical partners in architecting better brain health outcomes for our veteran population and beyond.

VA Innovation Ecosystem

By the time I met Dr. Rizzo, SoldierStrong's relationship with the VA had grown from one where SoldierStrong provided device donations to individual VA spinal center units, to something much more significant.

Back in 2014, I had the opportunity to briefly meet then-VA Secretary Bob McDonald, when we both spoke at a SoldierSuit donation event at the Palo Alto VA. In 2018, I took part in President George W. Bush's inaugural Stand-To Veterans Leadership Program. Over months of that program, I further developed my plan to serve America's veterans via SoldierStrong. Through that experience, I was re-introduced to Secretary McDonald, who saw the promise of SoldierStrong's program, and understood the "no DARPA for veterans" problem.

Secretary McDonald introduced me to the VA Innovators Network, a group of VA clinicians from across the country who were seeking innovative therapies, devices, treatments, and ways to support veterans who faced the toughest types of medical situations. That network, along with outside charitable and non-governmental partners, make up the VA Innovation Ecosystem.

The staff-level leadership within the Innovation Ecosystem embraced SoldierStrong and our mission quicker than any other bureaucratic network ever had. They understood that we were not asking the VA to support us, nor were we selling them anything. Rather, we wanted to work together with the VA to identify and deploy innovative technologies in order to benefit the veterans they serve.

The Innovators team helped us understand which individual VA medical centers around the country would embrace the type of technological revolution we saw coming, and which clinicians were ready to be forward-leaning and try new approaches to fixing a very old problem. In fact, the Innovators have become our personal guides as we navigate the many layers of the VA's bureaucracy. In more ways than one, they make sure that the solutions we advocate for reach the veterans who need them.

Price Tags

When I heard back from Dr. Rizzo after my trip to UT-Dallas, I was still braced for sticker shock. My hopes were already high for the promise this new approach held, but I was worried that the price tag would be prohibitive.

Skip told me he needed "a hundred" to get things going. In that $30 million had already been invested, my heart sank.

"A $100 million?" I asked. "That's beyond anything we can do."

"No, no, you don't understand," he said. "We need a hundred grand, not a hundred million."

It was hard to believe that after $30 million, this clinically promising tool that would intervene in one of the most lethal causes of veteran suicide, was only short another $100,000. I didn't know whether to celebrate the good news, or break down in tears at the idea that so many veterans had been neglected because of what seems like a rounding error when you get into numbers that large.

Skip made clear that the money would go directly to improving the system: making it more content-rich and flexible; lowering the overall cost; and providing new, more robust behavioral documentation features. These updates would expand its capacity for use as a research tool for PTSD, stress assessment, functional magnetic resonance imaging (fMRI), neuroscience research, and for pre-deployment resilience training. It would also begin the process of evolving military sexual trauma content, based on feedback that Dr. Rizzo's initial safety and feasibility trial acquired, documenting both safety and clinical efficacy.

All of this was in addition to putting BraveMind on a path toward the full transition as a best-of-breed tool for the safe and effective delivery of VRET.

Skip and his team had work to do. Their heavy-hitting list of goals included the following:

- Creating new scenario content and functional trigger stimuli.

- Optimizing the software for newer, lower cost, and higher fidelity VR headsets.

- Developing an online training resource for clinicians.

- Setting up an online registry.

- Implementing and improving the logging system for real-world use.

- Implementing after-action reviews.

- Improving various processes and menus.

- Exploring additional and emerging display and interaction hardware.

We didn't hesitate, and quickly agreed to fund the $100,000. In return, SoldierStrong gained the ability to purchase hardware and clinical training, install the software that Skip's team had created, and deliver an integrated product to the VA and other veteran-facing clinicians.

BraveMind Alliance

With a long list of things to do, and a complicated maze of hardware, software, and clinical considerations—as well as a large federal bureaucracy to navigate—I asked Skip if he would be willing to work with other academic institutions toward achieving some of those ends. He was almost offended that I had to ask. His response was immediately the right one: "Let's work with anyone who will help us deliver better results to our veterans," he said.

The first and most obvious partner was Dr. Sandi Chapman and her team at UT-Dallas's Center for BrainHealth. They had the clinical focus we needed, and already had the respect of and collegial relationship with Skip and his team. Sandi accepted our invitation to collaborate.

NEXT STEPS FORWARD

We searched next for a partner on the hardware side, and learned that Iowa State University's Virtual Reality Applications Center (VRAC) was the premier VR hardware lab in the country. VRAC's testing platform, the C6, is truly from the future, and represents the highest resolution, fully immersive VR environment in the world.

A long-time supporter and Iowa State faculty member—who also happened to be the father of an Army Green Beret, and a Navy SEAL—helped bring us into the fold. The VRAC played host to teams from other universities in the summer of 2019 to discuss ways to collaborate. Ultimately, they became our research and testing partner for hardware platforms and interfaces.

Rounding out our initial team was the Aging Studies Institute from Syracuse University's Maxwell School. This connection happened around the same time that I first learned the terrible statistic I shared in chapter 6—that more Vietnam vets had been lost to suicide than actually died in combat. Worse, the suicide rate among Vietnam vets had spiked, now that many of them had reached or surpassed retirement age. With these consequences in mind, we engaged the Aging Studies Institute to look seriously at the long-term impacts of unremitted PTSD.

These institutions continue to serve selflessly as part of our coalition of willing innovators—the BraveMind Alliance, which fostered SoldierStrong's BraveMind Program.

The BraveMind Program

Our goal with BraveMind is to reduce the number of veteran suicides that plague the country by coordinating between leading medical researchers, major universities, and multiple agencies of the federal government to provide revolutionary VR-based PTSD treatment.

New research and technologies continue to lead to more effective, affordable treatments for PTSD that can make meaningful, lasting impacts in the lives of veterans. Effective treatment of this underlying cause of many suicide attempts is helping to reduce the epidemic of veteran suicides across the country.

VR treatment shows promise in two key areas. First, it is clinically effective. Secondly, it minimizes the stigma around seeking PTSD treatment. For the last 10 years or so, VR in non-medical settings, such as video games and entertainment, has become more popular and culturally relevant. This, in turn, opens the doors for younger veterans to seek VR treatment in increasingly higher numbers.

Overcoming this stigma of seeking help is a huge development. In fact, many studies show that the stigma associated with getting help is one of the leading reasons why many vets refuse PTSD treatment. However, thanks in part to the popularity of gaming, VR therapy is a path that more and more veterans are willing to explore. In fact, one study found that if given a choice, 77% of potential patients would choose VR-delivered prolonged exposure, whereas one 23% would choose traditional talk therapy.[8]

A key part of BraveMind's efficacy is the therapist's ability to customize the world a patient experiences inside of the headset. Customizations closely match settings of bad memories, right down to the sights, sounds, time of day, and even smells. From the control panel, the therapist can put the patient in the driver's seat of a vehicle, or in a turret, for example. He or she can generate explosions, or make helicopters fly overhead as the patient narrates the story in the present tense.

"You're completely immersed in the moment," said Chris Merkle, a former Marine who tried VR therapy after serving three years in Iraq, and close to four years in Afghanistan. "You can feel it in your body when you talk. You just feel so tense. You don't get that normally unless you're in a really, really deep therapy session. VR therapy actually hands you your experience."

Confronting the memory head-on, over and over again, reduces the brain's response to it. Ultimately, the veteran in VR therapy begins to *control* the memory, and not the other way around.

Chris Merkle has become a major advocate for veterans, garnering community support for their transition, and reducing the stigma of mental health. As a Marine combat veteran, Chris openly challenges the stigma of mental health by sharing his battle with post-traumatic stress. His story is an extraordinary example of how VR technology like BraveMind has had a life-changing impact on so many veterans.

As proud as he is of his service to the nation, Merkle does not believe that service members should be defined by their past. "You fight for everyone's freedom, including your own. Back home, it's important to fight to regain or maintain your own happiness, and the American way of life."

BraveMind became the first program that meaningfully applied our SoldierStrong model to brain health: identifying, acquiring, and expediting the delivery of revolutionary technological advancement to meet a persistent and difficult problem. BraveMind continues to meet these standards as a clinically and culturally effective tool that reduces the stigma that can be just as lethal as any other component of this issue.

Today, a key part of BraveMind's success comes from the comprehensive dissemination of the system—literally getting it to the people who need this innovative and empirically validated approach. We believe we can continue to achieve our aim toward increasing adoption, availability, and effectiveness within clinical settings. All told, this will have a significantly positive impact on the lives of hundreds, perhaps thousands of service members and veterans.

As of this writing, SoldierStrong, working with the VA Innovation Center, has identified major academic VA clinics at which to begin deploying the BraveMind VR PTS protocol. As more resources become available, and as partnering professionals complete more clinical testing, we will continue to expand deployment of the protocol to other VA centers around the country.

Chapter 8
REACH

In the fall of 2019, I was introduced to Dr. Barbara Van Dahlen, who had just become the head of the PREVENTS task force. PREVENTS is one of those classic governmental acronyms—it stands for the President's Roadmap to Empower Veterans and End the National Tragedy of Suicide. Within that long name you find a vital mission, one which I was proud to join.

I was able to brief Dr. Van Dahlen about the BraveMind program and the promise it held. By the time of our first meeting, I had become accustomed to bureaucrats who were less interested in fixing problems than they were in following protocol and procedure. Van Dahlen, however, was a breath of fresh air: a woman of enormous experience and expertise who possessed enough professional humility to kick the doors open and accept good advice and ideas from nearly any source.

During our meeting, she heard and acknowledged the work we were doing and the model we had embraced at Soldier-Strong and BraveMind. We explained that while we didn't possess a magic bullet, we did hold a piece of the solution, and we wanted access to be able to advance it. She immediately agreed.

Our work with Dr. Van Dahlen and her PREVENTS task force would help lay the foundation for our future work in brain health. We quickly built a rapport. I respected her work, and liked her approach. Her willingness to consider new techniques and strategies was deeply refreshing.

She asked that I participate in assembling outside allies that could come together under the PREVENTS banner and look at ways to reduce the rate of veteran suicide. This included pulling together companies from the financial services industry, especially major Wall Street firms, that might be interested in partnering.

In October of 2019, I hosted Dr. Van Dahlen in New York City for a Veterans on Wall Street (VOWS) event. The VOWS program had started years earlier as a way to employ veterans who wanted to enter the private sector. Today, it includes a number of America's largest banks and Wall Street firms.

VOWS showed just how dedicated many financial services firms are to the idea that veterans possess employable skills, even if their resumes do not indicate a one-to-one transfer from military service to private sector employment. In fact, the resume issue was one of the major problems that VOWS began to solve. By the time we connected with VOWS, they were looking to extend their reach, and take on the very same veteran suicide issue we were trying to tackle. They were a perfect fit for the work we were doing with Dr. Van Dahlen and the PREVENTS task force.

Among key research findings into post-service happiness for veterans includes the fact that *earned success*—often from viable, ongoing and meaningful employment—is a major component to better mental health and sustained well-being. Just like any of us, veterans want to feel good about what they do for a living, where they do it, and with whom they work. They want and deserve salaries and benefits that help them see the links between what they do for a living, and what it means to care for themselves and their families. Without such links, it's too easy for many veterans to slip into depressive states that lead toward suicide ideation.[9]

The VOWS program has made tremendous strides in helping veterans see these links, and experience the positive benefits of meaningful, gainful employment. In their own way, VOWS has made important contributions to preventing veteran suicide. The program has replaced despair with a sense of purpose and achievement.

The day we hosted Dr. Van Dahlen and the VOWS banks in New York City marked the beginning of a discussion about how VOWS could support the work and mission of the PREVENTS task force—reducing, and eventually ending veteran suicide. As it turned out, this would be the first of many meetings that Dr. Van Dahlen and I would host together, including another just two weeks later, where we brought together a group of stakeholders to address public policy questions in Washington D.C.

We held this meeting under the aegis of SoldierStrong Access—a sister organization to SoldierStrong. Our goal was to push policymakers and stakeholders toward contributing better policymaking, starting with making sure they had a more in-depth understanding of the factors that contribute to veteran suicide ideation and attempts.

The distinction between SoldierStrong Access and SoldierStrong is key. SoldierStrong Access is a 501(c)(4) organization, whereas SoldierStrong is a 501(c)(3) charitable organization. As a 501(c)(4), SoldierStrong Access can identify, research, and educate policymakers and the public in ways a 501(c)(3) cannot. These types of organizations are built on action, and their reach extends beyond charitable efforts. This is critical, especially in our effort to motivate, innovate, and act. Dr. Van Dahlen was one of our very first high level, high profile policymakers who saw the value in this approach, and has been behind it every step of the way.

Our meeting was important for a number of reasons. First, we successfully rendered support for Dr. Van Dahlen by creating access to policymakers and financial services firms that wanted to help her mission. The meeting with a room full of policymakers also opened my eyes to the fact that issues related to mental health and wellness go far beyond those that veterans face. They were not the only community in need.

This line of thinking aligned with that of Dr. Sandi Chapman. She'd made it clear when we first met at UT-Dallas's Center for BrainHealth that a revolution in mental and brain health was coming to the country, just as a revolution in physical health came to the country in the previous century.

Sixty years ago, our habits—what we ate and drank; not wearing seatbelts; smoking; driving drunk; not exercising; etc.—were literally shortening our life spans. It wasn't because we were caught up in some kind of "macho culture." Rather, it was because, at the time, we possessed a limited public understanding of the medical science around how our physical and dietary habits impacted our health, for better or worse.

From the 1950s through the end of the 20th century, Americans began waking up to the risks associated with things like high cholesterol, too much saturated fat, smoking and drinking to excess, drunk driving, and other dangerous lifestyle behaviors and decisions.

This understanding started a revolution that shifted the way we ate, drank, worked out, and acted when driving. Among the consequences of these shifts include a marked increase in our life expectancy—moving the dial from the mid-60s to the mid-70s by the end of the century. The revolution in our collective understanding also softened, and even did away with many stigmas our culture had previously attached to certain lifestyle decisions and behaviors.

In Dr. Chapman's view, a similar shift regarding brain health is already underway. As science's understanding of the human brain, and what the human brain can do, continues to evolve, our culture will evolve with it. This will help do away with stigmas that have kept too many people from seeking help for far too long.

Our late October meeting led me to seriously consider how much of that cultural change was possible, and how SoldierStrong Access might think about affecting and even expediting it. Searching for ways forward—those vital next steps—sent me back to Dr. Chapman to continue this discussion.

I wanted to know if other leading figures in this space could help us think through and expand our contribution. Could we move beyond supporting veterans, and toward supporting the broader American population? What would it look like for our contribution to extend to the greater public? Could ours be a model that identified and rapidly deployed revolutionary technology to deal with long-term and seemingly intractable problems that plagued people from all walks of life, in every corner of this country?

NEXT STEPS FORWARD

In the early part of 2020, Dr. Chapman introduced me to Dr. Geoff Ling, one of the most impressive and kinetic human beings I have ever met. Deeply disciplined, and possessing a huge intellect, Dr. Ling is nonetheless gregarious, friendly, and most importantly, open to new people, experiences, and ideas.

When we met, Dr. Ling had been exploring an idea he called HARPA—Health Advanced Research Projects Agency. Essentially, it was a healthcare version of DARPA, focused on innovating the way to better health outcomes, including those related to brain health. This felt like more than a mere coincidence, considering that I had been working on an idea dubbed VARPA, which would mirror DARPA's approach, and help drive innovation in support of the VA.

HARPA was the brainchild of former NBC executive Bob Wright, and the Suzanne Wright Foundation, named in honor of his late wife. Dr. Ling and I immediately agreed that these ideas were strong and necessary. The overlap in our thinking was a clear sign that we were already philosophically aligned about addressing and solving long-held problems.

Dr. Ling and I started looking for ways in which we could collaborate, and how we could leverage our collective experience to advance a common solution set. We decided to work together and further our shared cause in ways that would support veterans, the VA, and the broader American culture.

It was clear to both of us that a large percentage of the population deals with issues related to mental health, brain health, and the stigma of seeking treatment every day. In our view—one that many experts share—there's a great divide between what science is discovering, and what the public knows and accepts. This divide may even be the health-culture problem of our time.

In April of 2020, just as the country was starting to go into COVID-19 lockdowns, Dr. Ling introduced me to Liz Feld of the Wright Foundation. The Wright Foundation is the host of HARPA.org, and this meeting was a major opportunity to expand our collaboration. Plus, the timing couldn't have been more extraordinary.

First, our ability to converse and move forward together in the early days of the pandemic is an example of what happens when innovation—Zoom calls—becomes commonplace. Without the technology to meet and converse, I'm not sure how far we would have gotten.

With regards to mental health, the ensuing lockdowns were about to introduce us to a level of mental health needs that we had never seen before. The disruption of our routines, coupled with issues of isolation and financial uncertainty saw major increases in anxiety, depression, and suicide ideation across the population. If ever there was a time to take steps toward building awareness around brain and mental health issues, we were in the midst of it.

Forming ReachStrong

To be in the presence of great minds like Drs. Ling, Chapman, and Van Dahlen felt like divine intervention. They were the right people at the right place and time. It was a chance to take our model, including everything we'd learned about deploying support, and apply it toward a much broader cultural need.

Our new goal reflected this shift: to educate the American public about improving brain health, and the importance of seeking treatment for issues related to depression, anxiety, and others that, when left untreated, lead to very dire consequences. In so doing, we sought to break down barriers and stigmas that traditionally block people from seeking help.

This set of factors is exactly why, in the first half of 2020, we created a new charitable organization called ReachStrong. As an ally and sister organization to SoldierStrong, ReachStrong's mission extended beyond the military, and aimed to apply our revolutionary change model in support of the broader American population.

BraveMind for Civilian Applications

The transition into providing solutions outside of the veteran community started us down a new, yet familiar, path. Once again, we were beginning from scratch, looking to create resources that would address an old and difficult problem. As we searched for better solutions, we kept our eyes on cutting-edge technology that promised revolutionary results for those who needed them the most.

However, what was different this time was that we had a beginning technology in mind. Leveraging the success of BraveMind in the veteran setting, we positioned ourselves as a conduit of sorts, in order to increase access to BraveMind for civilian PTSD cases.

Post-traumatic stress is not relegated to military experiences. It comes in many forms, often completely unrelated to combat. Many police officers, first responders, and frontline medical personnel deal with post-traumatic stress on a daily basis—they learn to bury their traumas, or shrug them off as "part of the job." Likewise, survivors of rape, sexual trauma, domestic violence, gun violence, and even automobile accidents carry PTS and PTSD throughout their lives.

Even for those who are aware of their post-traumatic stress, cultural stigmas related to brain and mental health remain. BraveMind offers promise in this regard, especially for younger generations, and people who are open to exploring and eventually embracing VR-based solutions.

Stigma is a uniquely cultural construct. Even with data, resources, and technologies at our disposal, it can be almost impossible to counteract stigma's grip. BraveMind does help, and we continue to look for additional innovations that will help us move the needle further. Still, the best way to deal with stigma is through the culture itself.

Cultures change, albeit slowly at times. Earlier, I mentioned the revolution in physical health that shifted our culture during the second half of the 20th century. It continues to hold great promise as a reference point as we consider changing the way we think about brain and mental health.

When we unpack our shift in physical health awareness, we find concrete and contemporary evidence that American culture is in fact open to new information, ideas, approaches, attitudes and—most importantly—changing habitual patterns. How did these changes take root during the last century? Quite simply, through public information and education.

As is almost always the case, the expertise and advanced knowledge breakthroughs in the scientific community took years to translate into new cultural understanding and norms. Take heart health, for instance. Heart disease remains one of the leading causes of death in the US; however, the rate of deaths due to heart disease has been halved since 1950.[10] The timeline that led to new perspectives and changed behaviors started slowly, but has continued to follow a progressively downward trend. It's easy to see that a game-changing cultural transformation took place with regards to heart health.

This is just one example that reconfirms something I hold true, and absolutely within our reach as Americans: cultural change is possible within a lifetime. What's more, this type of change is even easier at a time when we have so much access to communication technologies, and ways to spread knowledge and share information.

Finding New Ways to Communicate

If cultural change for brain and mental health begins with communication, then we needed to do the same. In mid-January, 2020, we launched ReachStrong: an online repository of information for those seeking better brain health resources.

Today, the ReachStrong site (ReachStrong.org) has become a hub where people can find an array of trustworthy news and information about brain and mental health, including factors, practices, and support for better mental health in their daily lives. It works in concert with our other activities to help knock down barriers, and create a pathway toward opening a better brain health future for millions of Americans.

We anticipate that ReachStrong will continue to be a go-to destination when it comes to accessing innovative brain health solutions—those that improve overall health, and also provide rapid pathways and access to new and transformational technologies, treatments, and cures.

Chapter 9

HORIZONS

A friend and colleague made an important observation recently: "Americans aren't about who we *are*," he said. "We're about who we can become. We also aren't about *where* we are. We're about where we *can* go."

I'd like to add the following: in America, it's only *impossible* to become something or go someplace if you *can't dream up* what the next horizon looks like. Sadly, doing so can be more difficult than it should be.

The story I'm living—the one I've just shared—started on the morning of September 11, 2001. That morning, I went to work, had my usual breakfast and coffee, settled into a typical morning meeting, and prepared for nothing special to happen. A few hours and thousands of steps later, nothing would ever be *usual* or *typical* again.

All I could do was focus on taking single *next steps* forward. I didn't have a grand vision or plan. But I left that day, and the experiences of that day, with a deep conviction that I had a calling to help others take next steps forward too—an insatiable appetite to give something back—for those who gave so much for us, and for those yet to come.

I didn't dare envision any of the innovations that would follow. I didn't know that socks for troops would become exoskeletons for veterans. I didn't know that these physically focused innovations would lead to transformational VR solutions to help heal the invisible wounds of war.

In no way did I think that I would be part of creating a model of innovation that would support the Veterans Affairs Administration, much less the broader American culture. The only horizon I saw that day was the one of getting safely home. Once I arrived, I wanted to help others get home as well—home to a better future.

What could we become, as a culture, a nation, a world, if we all moved in concert toward a similar horizon? I believe that this represents a mindset that most Americans share in their own personal way. I did not get here with a grand plan, just like I didn't get home with a plan. I just moved forward. My clarity of vision did not extend much farther than a few feet in front of me.

Today, I don't know where the next horizon is taking me, or taking us. But I do know that this horizon belongs to *all* of us. Just like I kept putting one foot in front of the other on 9/11, I will continue to do the same on this ongoing journey—taking one step at a time, until there are no more steps to take.

Of course, there will always be questions. More than 20 years since the events of 9/11, it's easy to wonder: What does the next horizon look like? How will we as a culture and a nation continue to put one foot in front of the other in order to get to our next horizon, and then beyond?

Horizons for Visible Wounds of War

We've seen the power of revolutionary medical devices for veterans who have served and sacrificed so gallantly on our behalf. The technical innovation that comes from some form of VARPA, or Veterans Advanced Research Projects Agency, is breathtaking.

To see a young veteran like Bryce Cherryholmes with a complete spinal cord injury stand up out of his wheelchair and walk again is extraordinary. Yet, I can't help but wonder what's next. What horizon is still out there? How will we step toward it?

Similarly, I envisioned the LUKE arm, one which DARPA collaborated with DEKA Research to invent.[11] The LUKE arm replaces the full range of motion from shoulder to elbow, to the rest of the hand and fingers, and returns to the recipient all of the wonderful complexities and movements that our arms provide. And yet....what does *the next horizon* look like? Does it involve *plugging* the arm into the central nervous system? Is it something else?

As next-gen science indicates, if the bundle of nerves that come through the shoulder are left intact when the amputation takes place, a device *can* be implanted into the central nervous system, and a recipient of a prosthetic arm can control it the same way you and I control our own: thinking, then doing, in a fraction of a second.

The next frontier for the exoskeleton, undoubtedly, will be more battery life, greater flexibility and maneuverability, and more practicality in the real world. In the near future, these exoskeleton devices *will* exist beyond rehabilitation centers; they will transform into everyday wearables. In fact, at some point in the future, people will wear them under their clothing.

And yet...

What a remarkable horizon it will be when we reach the idea that a person with a complete spinal cord injury *can* stand and walk again on her own, for a long period of time, without crutches or the aid of a physical therapist. This is indeed in our sights and within our grasp, if we are willing to go there, and take these next steps. Those who have sacrificed the use of their legs will regain the ability to move freely, as routinely and easily, as anyone who possesses the ability to walk can do right now.

You see, I believe that as revolutionary as it is for a person with a full spinal cord injury to walk, their ability to do so should not be confined to a clinical setting. We share an obligation to support people who have sacrificed their bodies for us. We must do more. It starts by lifting our eyes over the next horizon, and taking next steps forward until this vision becomes reality.

Horizons for Invisible Wounds

Perhaps even more exciting horizons exist in the area of brain health. For starters, VR treatment will be more broadly available for a larger cross section of underlying causes of PTSD in the very near future. Just imagine a world in which medical first responders who are subjected to post-traumatic stress factors on a daily basis, and the mental health consequences thereof, have VR protocols and software worlds into which they can enter and respond to the scenarios that cause trauma.

Imagine a world in which police officers in high-stress environments—who see humanity at its worst, and yet run *toward* the fray as others run away—can access technology that addresses their post-traumatic stress symptoms. Dr. Skip Rizzo has already worked with major American companies to address PTSD symptoms in American police officers, and early results are extremely promising.[12]

Today, when police officers go through de-escalation training, they experience a high rate of post-traumatic stress-like symptoms. This correlates with a vicious cycle that unfortunately plays out in American streets every day. First, officers find themselves on edge on account of their training; then, to combat the PTS symptoms they experience, they become desensitized to the humanity of the person on the other end of an altercation. This confluence creates more and more instances where officers, caught in fight or flight, abandon other de-escalation techniques, and pull their triggers.

And yet...what if de-escalation training in the near future includes PTSD remediation software that *re-sensitizes* officers to the humanity of the person on the other end of the interaction? What will *this* do for America?

Imagine a world in which growing up in a neighborhood or community where relations with police officers are always tense leads to PTSD-like symptoms. Maybe you don't have to imagine this world—maybe this is the world you know. There's an emerging body of scientific study that shows that citizens in such communities, especially people of color, experience PTSD-like symptoms simply on account of living in an environment where fear of law enforcement is normalized.

Now, imagine a world in which technological advancements and revolutions lead to community-based treatment that addresses the long-standing issues around race relations and policing. Such innovations may offer a third pathway that no one is discussing in the public discourse around policing and race—an entirely new way to support officers, individuals, and communites.[13]

To this I say: let's fund and deploy radical technological improvements in brain health, and mental health care and treatment—for law enforcement and for communities.

What if, in doing so, we discover that these treatments de-escalate violence, and begin to eradicate the problems that have stoked racial tensions in this country for decades?

Is technology a solution for every problem? No. Nor is that my claim. However, I do believe that these types of technologies can be extremely important and essential tools to possess and share in our collective American resource kit.

There's more. Consider the trauma that occurs from sexual abuse, whether in military or civilian environments. Among the many consequences of sexual abuse, we see brain health conditions that, clinically speaking, resemble post-traumatic stress disorder. Now: imagine a world in which VR for sexual trauma events is widely and regularly available in ways that help survivors of this trauma heal completely and quickly.

These are *not* far-off horizons. In fact, these innovations are visible today. However, we will never reach them by sitting around and looking. We must take the next steps. Sometimes, our steps will be painful; some steps might require that we go backwards first, then forward again. Yet, if every single day we wake up taking next steps toward those horizons, we will unlock this future.

As we pursue visible horizons, we open up opportunities that may currently be beyond our imaginations. And yet...once we stretch beyond what we can see and imagine, we will discover even greater innovations and opportunities that will improve lives, and change the way we relate to one another.

Why cling to old ways of doing things? Instead, I believe we must commit to being the best of our history: to go toward the frontier, then beyond, always pressing over the next hill, and past the horizon. That is the America I know—one in which we are still about where we *can* go, and who we *will* become. An America where the nearest horizon is simply the next, but not the last.

What's next has always been what interests us most. If you can see the next horizon, even if only in dreams or your mind's eye, you can arrive there. Then, you can take the next steps forward, one step at a time.

Photo Gallery 2

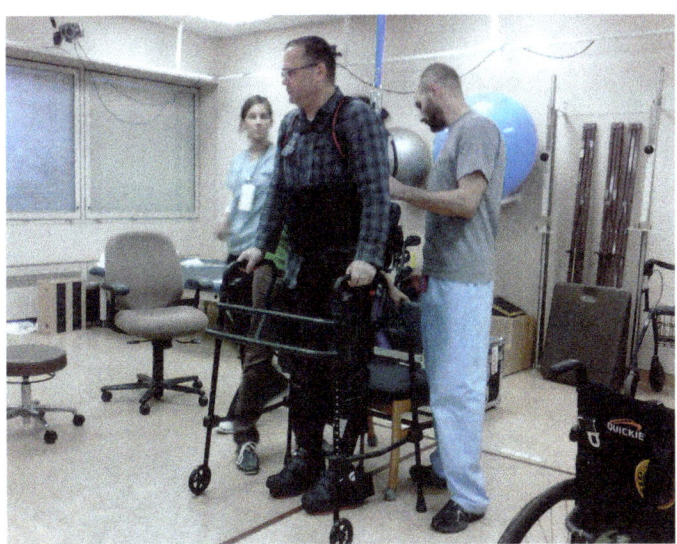

After being given less than a 5% chance to ever walk on his own again, Sergeant Ross worked valiantly to defy the odds with the help of regular physical therapy using the SoldierSuit.

Sergeant Matt Ross stands at the 50 yard line prior to kickoff at a Minnesota Vikings home game, needing only a cane for support.

NEXT STEPS FORWARD

Chris Meek testifies in front of Congress regarding the importance of delivering innovation in medical devices to our veterans. May, 2018.

During May 2018 congressional testimony, Chris shares a video of Sergeant Dan Rose walking with the help of the SoldierSuit.

Photo Gallery 2

Left-to-right: Secretary of Defense Chuck Hagel, Chris Meek, David Letterman and Navy Seal Commander Rorke Denver, at the annual Union League of Philadelphia event. October, 2018.

David Letterman, late night television icon and long-time supporter of our troops and veterans, stands with Sergeant Dan Rose at the Indy 500. May, 2017.

NEXT STEPS FORWARD

Sergeant Dan Rose stands with IndyCar driver Graham Rahal, Courtney Rahal, and Indy legend Bobby Rahal during the National Anthem before the Indianapolis 500 in 2018.

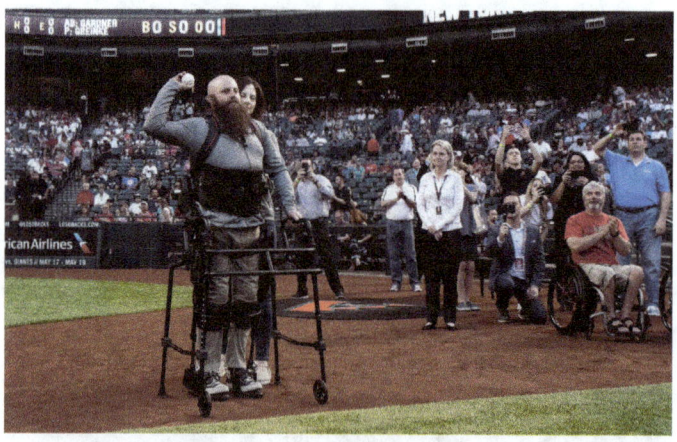

Sergeant Dan Rose throws out the ceremonial first pitch before an Arizona Diamondbacks game in April, 2019. For Rose, the first pitch represents a milestone in his personal recovery and battle back from a complete spinal rupture.

Photo Gallery 2

Chris Meek meets with NFL legend Roger Staubach during an October 2019 SoldierStrong fundraising event at the George W. Bush Presidential Center.

NEXT STEPS FORWARD

President Donald Trump announces the PREVENTS Roadmap on Veteran Suicide during a June 17, 2020 event at the White House.

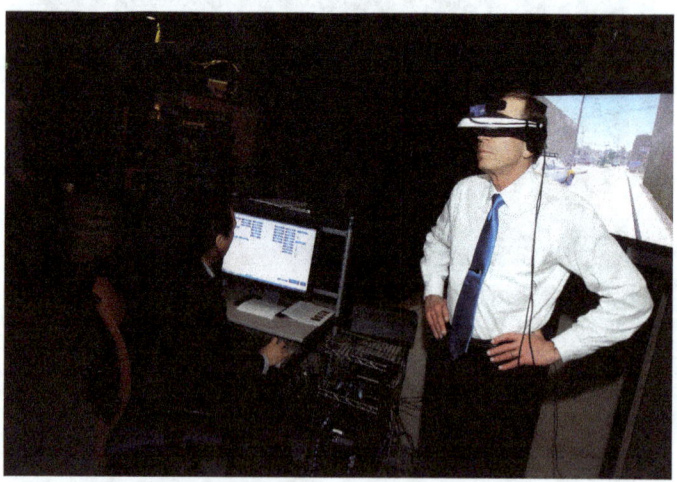

Retired US Army General David H. Petraeus explores the VR unit used as part of the BraveMind system.

Photo Gallery 2

A member of the US Armed Services explores VR therapy as General John F. Kelly looks on. General Kelly would later become White House chief of staff.

Dr. Skip Rizzo readies the simulator for a veteran preparing for a VR immersion demonstration.

The VR simulator takes this active duty member of the Armed Forces through a targeted immersion therapy session to help combat the effects of combat-related stress response.

ACKNOWLEDGMENTS

This book would not have been possible without the help and support of a great many people. I acknowledge and thank the following, though the list is partial:

My wife Christine Meek for her unwavering support.

My team of supporters who actively contribute time, guidance, and work on behalf of SoldierStrong, ReachStrong, and *Next Steps Forward*, including Eric Woolson, Christina Stroback, Jacob Krekura, and Gentry Collins.

Craig Pintoff, Chris Hummel, Jeremy Fountain, and United Rentals for their help resourcing our mission at SoldierStrong.

The Vince and Linda McMahon Foundation, WWE, and Linda McMahon personally, for their embrace and support of SoldierStrong's mission.

Graham and Courtney Rahal, who have been tireless advocates and supporters.

The scientists, innovators, and medical professionals who have guided our understanding and provided technical insight, including Dr. Barbara Van Dahlen, Dr. Skip Rizzo, Dr. Geoff Ling, and Dr. Sandi Chapman.

NEXT STEPS FORWARD

The men and women of the Department of Veterans Affairs who work to break through old ways of thinking and embrace a new and better path forward.

Our pioneering veterans who were early adopters of new technologies, including Dan Rose, Matt Ross, and Bryce Cherryholmes.

Martha MacCallum, whose early support for SoldierStrong's work offered national exposure and growth.

My editor Dave Jarecki and designer Lieve Maas, who took my story and made it readable and accessible.

Our men and women in uniform, whether military, police, or first responders, whose selfless service to our nation secures the blessings of liberty for us all.

ABOUT THE AUTHOR

Chris Meek is co-founder, chairman, and CEO of SoldierStrong, a 501 (c)(3) charitable organization that focuses on helping America's servicemen, women, and veterans take their next steps forward. He has been recognized for his work in philanthropy with the President's Call to Service Award (2011), March of Dimes Franklin Delano Roosevelt Outstanding Corporate Citizen Award (2012), Syracuse University's Orange Circle Award (2014), the ACT-IAC "Game Changer" Award (2020), and was named a "Face of Philanthropy" by the *Chronicle of Philanthropy* (2021).

In addition to Meek's work as a philanthropist, he is also a managing director and global relationship manager at S&P Global, Inc., covering some of the firm's largest clients. He holds a BA in economics and political science from Syracuse University, an MBA in financial management from Pace University in New York City, and an MPA from the Maxwell School at Syracuse University. He is a doctoral candidate in organizational change and leadership at the University of Southern California.

Meek serves as adjunct professor at the Maxwell School of Citizenship and Public Affairs at Syracuse University, where he teaches graduate and undergraduate courses on non-profit management and board governance. He shares his experiences and discusses resiliency, empowerment, and leadership through adversity on his weekly podcast, "Next Steps Forward with Chris Meek," via VoiceAmerica network's Empowerment Channel. *Next Steps Forward* is his first book.

NOTES

1. Page xvi: While the original title of this poem is "Judge Softly," Lathrap's poem later became known as "Walk a Mile in His Moccasins." As part of the public domain (published before 1927) I am grateful to share it as part of this book.

2. Page 15: You can search online for a quick reference to the Dow Industrial chart for all of 2001, such as through finance.yahoo.com.

3. Page 15: While the original Suspenders left Broadway a few years ago, you can find the bar at 108 Greenwich Street these days, near Trinity Church.

4. Page 43: This 2015 article and report provides insight into golden hour research and care: https://mtec-sc.org/wp-content/uploads/2017/08/ALT-2015-The-Golden-Hour.pdf; authored by Col Todd E. Rasmussen, Dr. David G. Baer, RADM Bruce A. Doll, and MG Joseph Caravalho Jr.

NEXT STEPS FORWARD

5. Page 45: There's a lot of information online about exoskeletons. Here's one example from a 2017 report, courtesy of NBC news: https://www.nbcnews.com/mach/innovation/robotic-exoskeletons-are-changing-lives-surprising-ways-n722676

6. Page 61: Articles related to suicide rates among veterans are unfortunately vast and varied. This study from the Department of Veterans Affairs focuses on troops deployed between 2001 and 2007: https://www.publichealth.va.gov/epidemiology/studies/suicide-risk-death-risk-recent-veterans.asp

7. Page 65: Navigating mental health can be difficult for many veterans, as the following article discusses: https://www.rand.org/health-care/projects/navigating-mental-health-care-for-veterans/mental-health-issues.html

8. Page 81: This vital data comes from the following: "Enhancing Exposure Therapy for Post Traumatic Stress Disorder: Virtual Reality and Imaginal Exposure with a Cognitive Enhancer." A randomized clinical trial. *Neuropsychopharmacology*. Contributors: Difede, J., Rothbaum, B.O., Rizzo, A.A., Wyka, K., Spielman, L., Reist, C., Roy., M., Jovanovic, T., Norrholm, S., Cukor, J., Olden, M., Glatt, C., & Lee, F. (under review).

9. Page 87: The following provides a trove of data related to health outcomes for many veterans: https://www.statista.com/topics/3488/veteran-health-in-the-us/#dossierContents__outerWrapper

Notes

10. Page 93: You can take a quick glance at US trends in heart disease, cancer, and stroke here: https://www.prb.org/resources/u-s-trends-in-heart-disease-cancer-and-stroke/

11. Page 97: You can learn more about the LUKE arm here: https://www.mobiusbionics.com/luke-arm/

12. Page 99: You can find an article on a recent study regarding game-based training for police officers here: https://www.rand.org/pubs/external_publications/EP68554.html; originally published: I/ITSEC 2020 Conference, Paper No. 20456 (2020)

13. Page 100: This article from *The Community Policing Dispatch* discusses the use of VR training to support community policing efforts: https://cops.usdoj.gov/html/dispatch/03-2018/vr_as_empathy_building_tool.html; 2018; John H. Kim.

To learn more about our mission and our work, please visit the following:

www.nextstepsforward.com
www.soldierstrong.org
www.soldierstrongaccess.org
www.reachstrong.org

www.ingramcontent.com/pod-product-compliance
Lightning Source LLC
Chambersburg PA
CBHW050330010526
44119CB00004B/114